Praise for Pat Pearson and *Stop Self-Sabotage*

"Stop self-sabotage and raise your Deserve Level if you want to transform your career, your relationships, and your life. Pat Pearson has written a profound and practical guide to rewriting your obsolete inner script, which keeps you stuck in roles that no longer suit you. Master the techniques in this gem of a book and watch your life-long dreams come into being."

—Jack Canfield, coauthor of *The Success Principles* and *The Key to Living the Law of Attraction*

"Self-sabotage is a STOP sign. My dear friend, Pat Pearson, shows you how to stop self-sabotage so you can go out and get the green lights in life and career. You can then have the extraordinary life meant to be yours and bring a lot of people along with you in the process. Congratulations in advance for reading this book, growing in self-confidence and self-esteem, and finding the way to move yourself and others forward. This is a must-read for career advancement!"

—Mark Victor Hansen, coauthor of *Chicken Soup for the Soul, Cracking the Millionaire Code*, and *The One Minute Millionaire*

"Every day we see powerful people tumble or know talented folks that never succeed. You might recognize one in the mirror! Time and time again, the reason is self-sabotage. In this insightful and illuminating work, Pat Pearson gives us the tools to recognize and overcome our personal minefields and step instead into the dynamic, rewarding lives we long for."

—Catherine Crier, former judge, host of Court TV's "Catherine Crier Live," bestselling author of *The Case Against Lawyers* and *A Deadly Game*

"Your inspiring and motivating seminar to our sales force of nine thousand people in Century 21 Real Estate was terrific. I am always amazed at how the sales numbers increase after your visits. Your book illustrates the way you can take a complicated subject like self-sabotage and have people understand what they are doing each day directly in opposition to their goals. To me, the biggest reason people don't achieve their goals is that they self-destruct along the way. Your book is a *must-read* for people who feel they could use some advice on how to win and keep on being winners for the rest of their lives. Good work!"
—Peter H. Thomas, founder of Century 21 of Canada, founder and chairperson of LifePilot

"Self-sabotage is as real as today's headlines. I'm in the business of helping people achieve peak performance, and overcoming self-sabotage is a first step. Pat Pearson shows you how to master this all-too-human tendency rather than letting it master you."
—James S. Logan, M.D., M.S., former Chief of Medical Operations, NASA Johnson Space Center

"Sometimes, no matter how hard you try, the 'big payoff' continues to elude you. Could it be that you are unwittingly holding yourself back because of limiting beliefs that are transparent to you? Pat Pearson provides the key to self-discovery and change that will unlock the door to abundance in your life forever!"
—Rosemary Redmond, president of Weekenders USA

STOP
Self-Sabotage

Get Out of Your Own Way to Earn More
Money, Improve Your Relationships,
and Find the Success You Deserve

PAT PEARSON, M.S.S.W.

New York Chicago San Francisco Lisbon London Madrid Mexico City
Milan New Delhi San Juan Seoul Singapore Sydney Toronto

The **McGraw·Hill** Companies

Library of Congress Cataloging-in-Publication Data

Pearson, Pat.
     Stop self-sabotage : get out of your own way to earn more money, improve your relationships, and find the success you deserve / Pat Pearson.
        p.   cm.
     ISBN 978-0-0-07-160319-5 (alk. paper)
     ISBN 0-07-160319-0 (alk. paper)
     1. Self-defeating behavior.   2. Success—Psychological aspects.   I. Title.

BF637.S37P43   2009
158—dc22   2008037711

1 2 3 4 5 6 7 8 9 10 11 12 13 14 15 16 17 18 19 20 21 22 FGR/FGR 0 9 8

ISBN 978-0-07-160319-5
MHID   0-07-160319-0

McGraw-Hill books are available at special quantity discounts to use as premiums and sales promotions or for use in corporate training programs. To contact a representative, please visit the Contact Us pages at www.mhprofessional.com.

This book is printed on acid-free paper.

This book is dedicated to Heather, Chris, Brad, Tim, and Jennifer (our fabulous children) and Brayden, Madeline, David, Julia, Andrew, and Johnny (our adorable grandchildren), with a special nod to the spouses of our children—Chris, Krista, and Cynthia.

May all of you believe in your own worth and Deserve Level and keep giving from the heart.

And at the beginning and end of every moment . . . there is my love, Steve.

Contents

Acknowledgments

IT TAKES A village to write a book! I want to honor the incredible talent this book has attracted. Brittany Holtzclaw has used her intelligence, dedication, and great loyalty to see this book into its final form. The words and soul of this book wouldn't have existed without the guidance of Hadley Fitzgerald. The good nature and can-do-ism of Stephanie Destatte while managing all of our other business has been exceptional. Thanks to Tonantzin Velazquez-Custodio for her grace and resourcefulness through this project.

My circle of friends has come through all the seasons of self-sabotage with me and contributed to the existence of this book. Don and Mary Kelly, on a beach in Hawaii, excited me so much by their enthusiasm that I refocused my writing efforts.

Thanks to the Literary Ladies of Newport Beach: Diana Wentworth, Debby Gaal, Mary Fletcher, and Mary Kelly, who loved me enough to point me in the right direction.

The fabulous girlfriends in Dallas: Susan Ellis, Ann Margolin, and Linda Dotson. Thank you for a lifetime of support and friendship.

Where would I be without the comfort, support, and love of my dear friends Jim Logan; Catherine Crier; Peter McGugan; Peter and Rita Thomas; Fred Margolin; Julie and Peter Hill; Mike Dotson; Mike James; Kyle Watts; Doug Fletcher; Ted Wentworth; Janet Cronstedt; Brenda Adriance and Shane Fox; Mike and Helen Cerletti; Maureen and Rob Chernick; David and Kathryn Waldrep;

Bob and Virginia Hilton; Chris Gaal; Roger and Lynn Tomalas; Ed and Linda Sherman; Al and Lisa Molina; Bob Henry; Katherine Glover; Debbie Cortes; Bobbi and Jerry Dauderman; Barb Middleton; Kathy Rasmussen; Toni Moltzan and Andrew; Nancy Stuckey and Kent Roberts; Gay Jurgens and Greg Reynolds; Gary and Joan Motley; Mark Victor Hansen; Jack Canfield; Tom McDonald; Leigh Erin Connealy and Patrick McCall; and Shauna Hicks, Jeff Harnar, and Barry Kleinbort, cocreators of *Therapy: The Musical*.

Thanks to my fabulous agent, Linda Konner, who immediately recognized the value of the *Self-Sabotage* material and never wavered in her commitment to get it published; and to Johanna Bowman, my editor at McGraw-Hill, who loved the book from the start and whose grace filled this project with joy.

PART I

Deserve Level

What Is It?

1

▼

The Fine Art of Self-Sabotage

EVERY MAN BORN HAS TO CARRY HIS LIFE TO A CERTAIN
DEPTH OR ELSE.
—Saul Bellow, *Henderson the Rain King*

SELF-SABOTAGE: WE ALL do it. Old or young. Rich or poor. Famous
or unknown. All of our talent, intellect, knowledge, and experience
cannot help us, because the enemy—the conspirator that whispers in
our ear and keeps us from our dreams—is ourself. But there is hope.
When we face our own fears and practice the techniques of change,
we can stop sabotaging our hopes and dreams.

"I just don't understand why I can't find a good relationship.
They all start out terrific and then . . . no one wants to make a commitment. Is it bad luck, or is it me? What am I doing wrong?"

"I'm in sales. I've made $45,000 for the last three years. I feel
stuck. Why can't I break through to make $50,000 or more?"

"I'm constantly on diets. I go up. I go down. But nothing ever
seems to truly work!"

"I work all the time at my home business, but can't seem to get
anywhere financially."

If you see yourself in any of these people—and I've talked with
all of them—or if there are some important goals you haven't yet
reached, *you are sabotaging*. You may not realize it (none of us do)
because sabotaging is unconscious.

If you could change one thing about your life, what would it be? Why don't you think you have it? Many people tell themselves it's bad luck, it's the economy, it's their mother, or that diets don't work. The truth is, each of the people I just mentioned—and every one of us as well—practices self-sabotage.

None of us wants second best. Our sabotaging causes us to do things that get in our own way, but the good news is that you can identify and correct those things. And it's easier than you ever thought.

One fascinating aspect of self-sabotage is that we often recognize it in our friends and loved ones but have a hard time seeing it in ourselves. The fact is, we worry most about sabotage in our children, friends, or mates. Will they make their careers work? Will they stop choosing the wrong relationships? Will they take better care of their health? These painful issues concern all of us.

Throughout our lives we've heard the message, "You can't have it all." Translation: if we really have—or become—everything we want, we will lose something important. Well, it's time to stop the old tapes and listen to something new. In this book you will find the stories of men and women who faced their limiting beliefs and moved around, over, under, or through their own self-imposed barriers to have the kind of life they wanted. I hope you'll find the stories not only inspirational, but motivational, and that you'll be sharing the story of your own triumph over self-sabotage very soon.

As a therapist listening to the unhappiness of my clients, I was often troubled that so many bright, interesting people weren't getting what they wanted in their lives. The kind of question I heard most frequently was, "Why is it taking me so long to get what I want?"

It's not because you don't deserve it.

It's not because you don't want it enough.

It's not because you aren't intelligent, attractive, or successful enough.

It's because you are *self-sabotaging*. You have conflicting thoughts and beliefs about actually having what you say you want. You are in resistance.

"I want to be a success in my career, but . . . "

"I want to lose weight, but . . . "

"I want a happy relationship, but . . . "

You are "yes, but"-ing yourself into self-sabotage. This book will teach you to name and change the sabotaging of your dreams and get out of your own way. By stopping self-sabotage, you will come to know you truly deserve what you most want to have or be in life.

And if you have even the tiniest fantasy that certain people are magically exempt from self-sabotage, please note: our culture is mesmerized by celebrities who sabotage themselves. The latest celebrity sabotage *du jour* makes headlines on the daily and nightly news shows. Beneath their glitter and glamour, celebrities are real people with personal struggles just like you and me. Their unresolved emotional baggage can wreck their lives and careers. It may be Louis Vuitton, but it's still baggage!

What Does *Deserve* Mean?

The *Webster's Dictionary* definition of *deserve* is "to be worthy of [merit]; deserves another chance; to be worthy, fit, or suitable for some reward or requital: to become recognized as they deserve."

My definition includes both an unconditional part—*being* worthy of what you want—and a conditional part—*doing* something to earn it. Your "Deserve Level" is composed of conscious and unconscious beliefs about what you deserve to be or have in your life. In other words, it is made up of a combination of four psychological issues:

- Your beliefs
- Your self-esteem
- Your self-confidence
- Permission from your past

And they all come together to form your Deserve Level script.

I'm using the word *level* in its metaphoric rather than its literal sense. Just as your IQ, your intelligence quotient, is an indicator of your level of intelligence, your Deserve Level is a gauge of the degree to which you believe you deserve to have what you want in various areas of life. Though your Deserve Level is based on the messages you learned as a child, Deserve Levels are self-chosen and can be changed.

You may consciously tell yourself you deserve to feel happy, financially secure, loved, and free of inappropriate guilt and negativity. But your Deserve Level unconsciously becomes your internal glass ceiling. You can't let yourself achieve or keep what you don't believe you deserve.

Important: Please Note

You deserve to get what *you* want and what *you* value—not what other people, according to their own standards, believe you should want and value—for instance, a certain status or income or type of relationship. Getting what you want requires you to make conscious and congruent choices that engage your heart and your desires. Once you make those choices, this book is here to assist you in breaking through any self-imposed limits on your dreams and desires.

Self-Sabotage

Self-sabotage is the way we regulate our Deserve Level to keep ourselves within our self-chosen—and surprisingly comfortable—boundaries. Self-sabotage is how we trip ourselves up when we're running to the finish line. No one is immune, and all of us do it to some degree.

In this book, you will learn how to stop self-sabotaging and raise your Deserve Level. You can't get and keep what you want if you don't believe you deserve it. We get what we believe we deserve. No more, no less. We never exceed our own expectations, at least not for long.

You were probably taught the myth that if you were kind, obeyed orders, and used your head, you would get what you wanted out of life. In other words, your good behavior would be a down payment on your heart's desires. Conversely, if bad things happened, it was probably your fault—"you should have thought about that before you did it"—and so you deserved what you got.

This concept of earning or controlling all the outcomes of our lives is flawed. You cannot control major acts of God, the economy, or other people's feelings. That's the bad news.

The good news is that you are in charge of your own choices, feelings, and behaviors. That is where you can make a change.

As opposed to one-time events which, while unpleasant, do not recur, self-sabotage is a repetitive *pattern* that shows up in the guise of various events and people and diets and experiences. The net outcome is that you're chronically frustrated and unhappy about where you are.

As a psychotherapist, I work every day with people who want more in their lives. In the early years of my practice, when I noticed some people never seemed to get what they wanted, I tended to think, "Well, they didn't commit to therapy, didn't really work for it." Yet some of them worked really hard and still were not able to achieve what they wanted in their lives! With all their genuine motivation and sincere application of techniques, why didn't they improve?

The answer, I came to believe, is that *they didn't believe they deserved to get what they said they wanted.* There was some kind of invisible shield between their wants and their ability to satisfy those wants. Every day they ran full speed into this shield, fell down, picked themselves up, then did it all over again! This repetition was the most frustrating pattern in their lives.

Then I became aware of this pattern in my own life.

My Own Self-Sabotage and Deserve Problem

I grew up in a small Midwestern town in the standard 1950s and '60s way. My father was a successful national book salesman. My mother was a college professor.

My father had very high standards; he was very critical and difficult to please. He was charming, handsome, and witty, and seemed fun and accepting to those outside the family. Behind closed doors, however, he was demanding and perfectionistic and led me to feel I could never quite measure up.

My mother, on the other hand, was loving, supportive, and accepting. Dad would yell and she'd cower; then she'd come back to me later and reassure me I was good and loved. Out of this mix I developed my own patterns of self-sabotage.

I first experienced my own Deserve Level issues after college. Near the end of my senior year I fell in love with my young, brilliant college professor. He was everything I believed I wanted in a romantic partner; I was truly swept off my feet.

After graduation he suggested I travel with him and his family to Europe for the summer, then move to Boston to be with him when he started his new job at Harvard. I said yes without a second thought. Surely I had won the emotional sweepstakes; Cinderella had nothing on me!

Friends and family had expressed concern about both my prince and the demanding nature of his plans. But I joyfully went off to Europe and on to Boston, ignoring their cautions about the man as well as the move.

Within weeks I was living in a new city with no job, no friends, and a newly printed degree in political science. No one in Boston was particularly impressed with my undergraduate degree, so I ended up selling clothes in Harvard Square.

Then one night I found the professor with another woman, and I was shattered. It was one of those moments when the world stops, when a single experience is stamped forever in your memory and changes your entire perception of the world. I had believed we'd be married and live happily ever after in Cambridge, but my personal fairy tale had vanished. After a very intense scene full of accusations and tears, I called my parents, and they sent me the money to move back home.

I went back in despair, and for several weeks I sat: literally sat. I was in excruciating emotional pain, had no interest in friends or family, lost weight, felt nauseated, and couldn't sleep; or if I did fall asleep, the nightmares were exhausting. I walked around with my shoulders pulled almost to my ears, like a tortoise trying to withdraw her head into her shell. My neck and back were in constant spasms from muscular tension. I was deeply depressed.

My family became very concerned. The daughter whom they had raised and spent thousands of dollars educating was becoming a vegetable in her room. They took me to internists, family friends, clergymen—anyone they thought might help snap me back to normal functioning. I wouldn't be helped. They even began talking about surgery because my shoulders literally seemed frozen and would not come down from around my ears.

Finally, something in me snapped, and I said, "Wait a minute. I think this is all emotional."

I remembered a psychotherapist I had met through friends at college. I called him and we talked on the phone. That phone call, which became my first therapy session, changed my life.

During the call I started to cry and talk about the dream I had lost. After the call, my shoulders came down about half an inch.

I called again the next night. This time I got angry and talked about betrayal and rage. My shoulders dropped another half-inch.

By the end of the week the tension and pain were gone from my shoulders, neck, and back. I felt saved. I knew that what happened to me in Boston was something I never wanted to experience again.

I decided the only way I could make sure it didn't happen was to learn everything I could about myself and my pattern for choosing men. I returned to Dallas and entered therapy with the man who had helped me on the phone.

In therapy I reviewed all my past romantic relationships, and that's how I discovered I had a wonderful ability to sabotage myself by choosing witty, charming men who would never commit to marriage. I fell in love with their "potential" and completely denied the reality that they didn't want the same outcome I did. It always became my goal to figure out ways to make *them* change—and once they did, my worth would surely be confirmed.

When they continued to resist my attempts to change them, I simply tried harder. Yet not one of those relationships was ever changed by my attempts at psychic urban renewal. In time I came to understand that, at a very fundamental level, I didn't believe I deserved what I'd been seeking.

Raise Your Deserve Level

Before you can have more in your life, you have to follow the ancient maxim "Know thyself."

That means making changes at a deep and profound level. You • can make some of those changes quickly and easily. Others will take longer, will not be easy, and will require a commitment to the evolutionary process that is change.

The rewards can be summed up in one sentence: *you can have more in your life than you have ever had—and truly enjoy it!*

You are the only person who is entitled to decide what that "more" will be. Perhaps it's more income, more loving relationships, more of a sense of safety, more spiritual development, or more health and energy.

You already know about the stress and pain of deeply wanting someone or something, yet feeling chronically blocked from getting it. There is such frustration in trying, and the painful irony is that trying doesn't work anyway. You probably know someone right now who is *trying* to quit drinking, lose weight, or give up a destructive relationship. The only way to stop feeling the anguish of that frustration is to fully understand and resolve the "how" and the "why" of sabotaging behaviors.

Your final decision regarding what you deserve is influenced by all your beliefs and feelings, conscious and unconscious. There are specific Deserve Levels for every area of your life: love, work, friends, health. Paradoxically, it is possible to have a high Deserve Level in one area (career, for example) and a low Deserve Level in another (for example, relationships).

Low Deserve Levels can live inside of us no matter how rich or famous we are. Elizabeth Taylor is a perfect example. She made millions as a successful movie star yet had seven failed marriages (relationship self-sabotage). There can also be a domino effect if one area is seriously out of balance. Robert Downey Jr.'s alcoholism and drug addiction (health self-sabotage) almost ruined his movie career. One sabotaged area can topple an entire life; conversely, one area of sabotaging can be dealt with effectively if the others are in balance. This is why some people handle a career loss well and others don't.

Figure 1.1

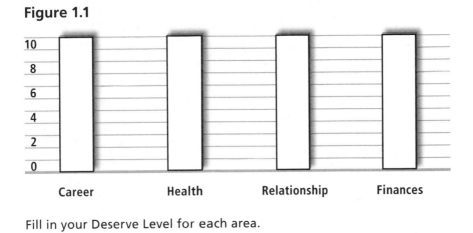

Fill in your Deserve Level for each area.

Use this bar graph (see Figure 1.1) to rate your Deserve Levels on a scale of one to ten, with ten being the highest rating. Your rating should be subjectively based on what you feel right now about your life.

Look at the area you rated the lowest: that's the Deserve Level with which you need the most help.

You Deserve Life's Good Things

You were born with the fundamental right to believe the best of yourself. This entitlement is basic to every human being. Somewhere along the way, though, we begin to have doubts about just what and how much we deserve.

Babies have no question about their right to be loved or held. When they're hungry or wet, they scream to let the world know of their basic needs. They feel no need to apologize or justify—they just feel it! They ask for what they want and respond spontaneously when they don't get it.

Then something happens. It happens subtly and over time, but it happens. Our innate sense of being worthy to express our feelings and needs starts to get lost as we mature. Instead of believing we deserve love just for "being," we lower our self-esteem and try to earn approval and love by "doing." We begin to think we must earn love, and so we give up our real feelings to meet the approved image.

A two-year-old confidently attempts almost anything. He may not accomplish it, but he will darn well try if the adults in his life don't prevent him. As we get older, we start to shrink our beliefs about our own abilities. Somehow the other guy can make the higher grades, get the big sale or promotion, go after the advanced degree, win the beloved. But not us.

These feelings and beliefs sabotage our confidence and self-esteem. They drain our psychic and physical energy. They resemble a low-grade infection that's too subtle to diagnose, making us feel defeated before we begin. We may be willing to give it that old college try, but in our hearts we know we're *only* trying, not succeeding. Again: we never exceed our own expectations, at least not for long.

Cliché though it may be, change does take time. Deserving more means you will expand your beliefs, your feelings, and your spirituality—in other words, you will expand the limits of your Deserve Level. It's an inner journey, a unification, that becomes an outer reality. This is not magic. It is a true, conscious, and purposeful alignment of your beliefs, choices, feelings, and thoughts.

With my clients, and in my own life, I have learned that we don't allow ourselves to have what we want until we believe—truly believe—that we deserve it.

Specific wants differ from person to person. One wants to find a life partner, another to build a fortune, another to be free from anxiety, another to make a marriage work. Regardless of the wish, there's often a vast chasm between what we say we want and what we believe we deserve.

Our psychological comfort zones mediate our Deserve Level limits. If we achieve beyond our comfort zone, we face a choice:

- To give away what we have achieved
- To increase our Deserve Level limits to encompass this increase

Self-sabotage is the operational way we keep ourselves within our self-chosen limits. This is why people can lose fifty pounds and put seventy back on—or live happily at their new weight.

The Psychological Deserve Point

Just as each of us has what's been identified as a *metabolic set point* that controls our bodies, we each have in certain areas of our lives a *psychological set point* that determines our Deserve Level. And just as the metabolic set point operates on an unseen and unconscious level, our psychological set point also operates underground. One set point has a profound effect on our bodies, the other has a profound effect on our minds—and our behavior. The good news is that, similar to the way the metabolic set point can be altered through diet and exercise, the psychological set point can be altered through awareness and a willingness to change. Both can be improved to new levels by identifying and changing the input that created them.

Since we tend to live out the reality of our constraints rather than soaring with the vision of the possible, we have to achieve congruency between what we want and what we believe we deserve in order to have a full, happy life. Our personal expectations form the bridge between what we want and what we deserve.

Negative Expectations: I don't deserve it. (I'll sabotage getting it or I'll sabotage keeping it.)

Positive Expectations: I deserve it. (I'll facilitate getting it and enjoy it once I achieve it.)

Listen to yourself talk about your dreams or desires. Do you say "I deserve to have this," or do you make other, negative statements?

Before I increased my Deserve Level in relationships, I had a low-level dread and expectation that they would not work out. I *wanted* to find the man of my dreams but I *expected* that the relationship wouldn't last. This expectation was based on my lack of self-esteem, my belief system, and my personal history. Getting involved with the wrong man had led to a dreaded outcome so many times that this outcome had begun to feel like my fate.

We cannot always be aware of our unconscious beliefs, but we can see the evidence of them by what we have in our lives. If we change our Deserve Level, we begin to expect to get what we want—and it's at that point we can become *congruent* with *wanting* and *deserving*. This congruency leads us to actualizing our dreams.

The Spiritual Side of Deserving

There is also a deeper, spiritual sense of deserving—the feeling that we're worthy of the joy and happiness a well-lived life can bring. Every individual's birthright is that of knowing she or he is loved by the Source (God) of all creation.

But due to the fear of not being enough, of being unworthy, the normal creativity of individuals is often blocked. It is somehow easier to be unworthy, to act from a state of not deserving, to perceive yourself as being less; and the Deserve Level of most people is limited by these self-perceptions.

Part of the spiritual journey, the spiritual quest, is to renounce the ease of opting out. It takes a certain level of spiritual courage for you to feel and believe you deserve more. You will need to renounce the personally and culturally imposed notions of limitation and embrace the knowledge that there's an inherent abundance in this life.

As a spiritual being in a human life, you have the birthright to accept that you are loved unconditionally. You have the birthright to accept that you have a unique purpose in living, and therefore your life experiences can reflect your purpose, beliefs, and truth.

All of us deserve to be happy, to have love, to have fullness in life. And surprisingly few of us have been able to achieve this. Suffering through abuse, regret, rejections, abandonment, and losses all affect the ability of our consciousness to see and feel that our Deserve Level can be balanced. Unworthiness lurks in the unconscious mind and turns into a deep-seated belief about the very nature of one's life.

You can raise your Deserve Level to accept your right to be happy, worthy, and successful. You have the right to create opportunities for fulfillment and the right to choose to live in joy and peace, rather than in the hostilities that come from fear.

This is a Deserve Quest. When your deepest wounds are integrated, they become your strongest powers. That means you have to go inside; you have to make that single, most important journey to reclaim your dreams and desires—and, in so doing, raise your Deserve Level. That's what this book will teach you to do.

▶ Exercise: Finding Your Deserve Level

What do you believe you deserve in your relationships?

_____

_____

_____

What do you believe you deserve in your health (including weight)?

_____

_____

_____

What do you believe you deserve in your finances?

_____

_____

_____

What do you believe you deserve in your career?

_____

_____

_____

In which of those areas do you want to raise your Deserve
Level?

_____

_____

_____

2

▼

What's in It for Me?

WHEN WE ARE NO LONGER ABLE TO CHANGE A SITUATION
WE ARE CHALLENGED TO CHANGE OURSELVES.
—Victor Frankl, *Man's Search for Meaning*

AFTER REALIZING WE all self-sabotage, the question becomes: how often and how severe is it?

Almost everywhere we turn, we can see varying degrees of self-sabotage in media celebrities, in our friends, and in ourselves. It is the single most frustrating part of everyone's life, and it's what we worry about most in the lives of those dear to us. We see their choices not getting them what they want and deserve in life. We hear the questions tossed around on the phone, at the dining-room table, and in our hearts:

"Why does my best friend keep picking the wrong men?"

"Why doesn't my brother ever get promoted?"

"Why can't my father lose the weight that's hurting his health?"

"Why am I not making more money?"

Self-sabotage is the emotional straitjacket on our behaviors and our feelings. It binds us tightly with negative subconscious straps that keep us from reaching out and grabbing what we most yearn for and deserve in life. You can throw off that straitjacket forever.

To put it another way: you can stop hitting your head on the internal glass ceiling of your own beliefs. That seems a little perverse—why in the world would we keep doing that? The answer is, we do it unconsciously, not intentionally. It's called resistance.

Fear: The Fatal Attraction

As humans, we naturally fear that what has already happened to us will happen again. The problem with this is that we allow our past to predict our future. For instance, if we were abandoned as children, we'll likely fear abandonment as adults. So, fearing more abandonment, we will "protect" ourselves by abandoning someone before they abandon us.

If we fear someone will reject us, we'll reject ourselves first. We'll stop ourselves from approaching that person and then rationalize it by proclaiming: "He (or she) won't be interested, so why bother?"

If we fear intimacy, we'll date—or even marry—people we can never get close to.

If we fear success, we'll make sure we never get it. Or, if we finally attain success, we'll make sure we do something to sabotage it.

Our unconscious memories of fear and pain make us tremendously prone to self-sabotage. Paradoxically, by *focusing* on our past fears and pains, we increase the likelihood of re-experiencing them.

If all our fears were real, it would be easy to understand why we so readily submit to them. But the vast majority of our fears are imagined, no more real than the boogeyman hiding in our childhood closet.

But because energy and action follow our thoughts, the more we think and obsess about our fears, the more we make them real. One of my friends aptly described the crippling effect of fear this way: "Fear is that little dark room where negatives are developed."

Chris is a male actor who was struggling to get noticed for roles in the film industry. Every time he got a serious callback for a part, he'd go out the night before and get drunk. He'd arrive hung over and unshaven and would inevitably fail to get the part. His fear of rejection made him set himself up to be rejected.

As Gerald Jampolsky says in his book *Love Is Letting Go of Fear*:

The world we see that seems so insane may be the result of a belief system that isn't working. The belief system holds that the fearful past will extend into a fearful future, making the past and the future one. It is our memory of fear and pain that makes us feel so vulnerable. It is this feeling of vulnerability that makes us want to control and predict the future at all costs.

The paradoxical nature of fear is that by focusing on what we fear, we increase the chances of its happening. By trying to control our lives so that something won't happen, we give energy to the possibility of its occurrence, and thus we sabotage our dreams.

Here's a story about fearing the worst. While raiding the refrigerator for a midnight snack, John turned around to find a burglar in his kitchen. After recovering from his initial fright, John exclaimed: "Before you rob me, I'd like you to meet my wife." The burglar looked at him warily, thinking this was a trap, and John said: "She's been expecting to see you here in this house every night for thirty-five years, and I'd hate for her to miss you!"

Most of our fears are imaginary. They have their own set of eyes, able to see what isn't really there. The problem is that fears become neurotic when we take them too seriously. We energize and infuse them with their own reality when we worry and replay those old negative tapes.

As Henry David Thoreau said: "Most men lead lives of quiet desperation and go to the grave with the song still in them." That desperation is constantly being fed by our fears and funneled into our self-sabotaging behaviors. So, we're all challenged to be in charge of our fear rather than letting it dictate to us.

In Frank Herbert's science-fiction classic *Dune*, there is a wonderful mantra for dispelling fear:

I must not fear. Fear is the mind-killer. Fear is the little death that brings total obliteration. I will face my fear. I will permit it to pass over and through me. And when it has gone past, I will turn the

inner eye to see its path. Where the fear has gone there will be noth-
ing. Only I will remain.

We must face our fears and reframe our self-sabotaging thoughts instead of being victims and feeling helpless. Words like "I can't," "I should," "I'm not good enough," and "It's terrible" need to be changed to focus on more empowering beliefs like "I choose," "I'm worth it," and "I can handle this!"

In her wonderful book *Feel the Fear and Do It Anyway* (the title says it all!), Susan Jeffers calls attention to *fear truths*. She says, "Pushing through fear is less frightening than living with the underlying fear that comes from a feeling of helplessness." Even more important, she says "I can handle this!" is the universal declaration to help keep us empowered in any situation: "If you knew you could handle anything that came your way, what would you possibly have to fear?"

Sabotage Strategies

In a business as well as in a personal context, the word *strategy* is regularly thought of as a conscious, positive plan for moving forward and gaining an advantage. In this book, however, I'm giving the unconscious mind its due. I'm acknowledging the surprisingly powerful ways it can call up an old image of you and plug you back into an old script, so that you think and behave in a historical and reactive way rather than in a way that's contemporary and proactive.

In other words, as long as your unconscious mind is allowed to do the assessing and strategizing in your life, it becomes the spoiler—able to generate a continual supply of self-sabotaging "strategies" that turn roads into ruts in your life. My goal is to get you to recognize and become conscious of the strategies you use so you can change them once and for all.

There are five common sabotage strategies that grow out of our focused fears and either drive us into negative action or send us running away from our desires. As a result, we repeatedly adjust our lives to stay within our self-chosen limits. Unless and until we understand these strategies, it's almost impossible to raise our Deserve Levels.

1. Resignation

"Deep down I don't believe I deserve it, so I won't even go after it."
"I don't like to get my hopes up. Then, if I don't get it, it won't hurt
so much." This leads you to *create your own reality.*

Cynthia is a beautiful, bright attorney with everything going for
her. She's a balanced woman with many interests and friends. She
divides her time between a successful law practice, volunteer work
with abused kids, and many singles groups and activities.

Extroverted and entertaining, she attracts many men and gets
asked out a lot. That's when her sabotage begins.

She gets into a relationship and really wants it to work. For about
six months she is passionately involved with that partner. Then, like
clockwork, she decides he is going to leave her. She won't return the
man's phone calls, talk with him, or discuss the problem. She simply
withdraws all affection and attention. She freezes emotionally and
resigns herself to being alone again.

As Cynthia says, "I don't want to be one of those women who
just hangs on long after the love is gone." What she wants is a good
relationship. What she has is a long list of ex-boyfriends! Her sabotage strategy is *resignation.* She gives up before she really begins. Her
past experience with her mother's six marriages created her belief that
no relationship will last.

2. Denial

"I won't pay any attention to this problem. It will just go away." "It's
not really that important or significant." In other words, you are
saying "I deny responsibility" and "I blame others for my problems."
This leads to *living out the Peter Principle.*

By any standard, Bill was a great insurance salesman who earned
more commissions than anyone in his agency. His dream was to have
his own company, to have the challenge and fun of running his own
business. When his agency head decided to retire, Bill bought the
agency.

Eight months later, Bill could be found staring blankly out the
window, yelling at his salespeople, and generally ruining everyone's

day. The daily management of the office was killing him. He was a stellar salesperson, but he was not a manager. He loved interacting with people but hated planning and detail. When his paperwork began to backlog, he became rigid, compulsive, and irritable. He was in denial about his inability to handle the administrative side of the business. He felt overwhelmed, spent his time doing unproductive tasks, and sabotaged himself by refusing to delegate or to ask for help.

The sales force, uneasy without effective management, was in mutiny. Bill kept denying the reality of reduced premium flow and declining profits, hoping his "luck" would change.

He lost $250,000 before admitting he was in the wrong part of the business. He still could have implemented changes that would have saved his business, but his sabotage strategy of *denial* kept him from acknowledging reality. What he would not see, he could not change.

3. Throwing It Away

"I get it, but then, since I don't really deserve it, I blow it." "I throw away my dreams." This sets the *roots of failure* solidly into the ground of one's future.

Susan had a rare gift for connecting with people. After selling hard just to get the job, she made $60,000 during her very first year in radio sales. She had arrived.

But her "arrival" soon made her very nervous. Maybe other people at the station wouldn't like the successful Susan. That's what had happened to her in school—it seemed that every time she got an award, the other kids pulled away from her.

Susan had grown up poor. No one in her family had ever made more than $20,000 a year, so it was hard for her to believe she was making three times that amount. Her family was initially proud of her success, but soon began making veiled comments about her seeming "uppity" and "getting fancier" than the rest of them.

During her second year she made $40,000. She says, "I'd like to make more, but I just feel uncomfortable."

Susan had success, but she threw it away. At some level she didn't believe she deserved it; or on a deeper level, she feared it might cost her the love and goodwill of her family, toward whom she had the oddest feeling she was being disloyal.

4. Settling for Less

"I want it, but I'm not really good enough, so I'll settle for less." "I won't try very hard because I probably won't get it anyway." This proves the old *nothing ventured, nothing gained* maxim.

David is a shy, intelligent CPA with a large accounting firm. He wants to have a relationship but becomes fearful every time he wants to meet a lady. He says, "I've always been bashful. I just don't know what to say to the women I meet—so I don't meet them. I stand in the corner at parties and study my feet."

After we talked about the self-sabotaging nature of this old ritual, he decided to take the plunge and actually meet someone at a party he'd been invited to. The next week he came into my office feeling very self-satisfied. When I asked what had happened, he said he'd met someone at the party. "I walked into this party and decided I'd look over all the women there and select the one I most wanted to meet. I picked her out and then I completely avoided her! But later I ended up talking with the woman standing next to me—she was avoiding people, too."

David did meet someone and did make some advances, but he was still *settling for less* than he said he wanted.

5. The Fatal Flaw

People identified with this strategy may be taking all the right steps, but they have a crucial personality problem—perfectionism, procrastination, anger issues, narcissism—that eventually undoes all their best efforts. To others they often seem to be *the perfect pain in the neck.*

Brilliant, talented, a vice president of a large multinational company, Carl was a man on the rise. He did his work flawlessly, came up with innovative techniques, and turned in a superb performance on every job. Carl was virtually perfect. The president of his division respected and liked him.

With the employees, however, there was an entirely different scenario. Carl drove everybody crazy with his perfectionism. He corrected people's slightest imperfections, pointing out ways they could improve everything from their memo writing to their exercise programs. He constantly interrupted people and debated the smallest points.

Eventually and inevitably, wherever Carl went in various companies, he left a wake of angry people behind him. Despite his competence, his perfectionism was a *fatal flaw* with regard to realizing his ambitions in his field.

Cynthia, Bill, Susan, David, and Carl are all bright, competent people who each managed to find a way to sabotage an achievement they held dear. Their unconscious sabotage strategies have in common an underlying, unconscious sense of *not deserving* the sought-after goal, which prevents them from reaching or holding onto the desired outcome.

As someone ruefully said: "I always figure out a way to snatch defeat from the jaws of victory!" He is not alone! Every day of the week intelligent, motivated people do themselves in with self-sabotage, using strategies about which they may be completely oblivious at a conscious level. Even the current rich-and-famous have struggled with their own self-sabotage strategies. Just think back to the antics of Bill Clinton, Martha Stewart, Michael Jackson, Mel Gibson, and the current celebrity saboteur.

How do *you* self-sabotage? How are you limiting your life's success, and by how much? To find some of those answers, take this quiz.

▶ **Exercise: Sabotage Warning Signals**

1. You fail over and over again in a certain area (weight, exercise, love, or success).

   YES   NO

2. You always get close to the goal but don't ever achieve it—
   "always a bridesmaid, never a bride." (This is pre-achievement
   sabotage.)

   YES   NO

3. You reach the goal and then lose all interest in keeping it. (This
   is post-achievement sabotage.)

   YES   NO

4. You feel uncomfortable, anxious, or worried about a recent success. You can't enjoy it. Comfort returns when you give it away.
   (This is throwing-it-away sabotage.)

   YES   NO

5. You tell yourself, "I don't deserve it." (This is self-esteem
   sabotage.)

   YES   NO

6. You tell yourself, "I can't do it." (This is self-confidence sabotage.)

   YES   NO

7. You deny responsibility for your own life—you blame others.
   (This is denial sabotage.)

   YES   NO

8. You don't believe you can have the prize or dream you want;
   you give up without really going for it. (This is resignation
   sabotage.)

   YES   NO

9. You consistently settle for less than what you really want. (This
   is settling-for-less sabotage.)

   YES   NO

10. As you get close to the goal, a fatal flaw (like alcoholism, depression, or perfectionism) creates a negative outcome. (This is fatal-flaw sabotage.)

    YES   NO

11. You don't want to be or do better than your parents, your spouse, or your friends. (This is a lack of permission from your past.)

    YES   NO

12. You are a rescuer and give up your own desires to help others, thereby never reaching your goals. (This is fatal-flaw sabotage.)

    YES   NO

If you have:

> **One to two "yes" answers:** You are mildly self-sabotaging; your beliefs and feelings are putting a hold on your forward motion. You are driving with the gas and the brake on at the same time. Learn to release the brake and see how fast you reach your goals!

> **Three to six "yes" answers:** You are moderately to severely self-sabotaging. You're significantly restricting your ability to get what you deserve to achieve in your life. Isolate your specific sabotaging behaviors and come up with a plan to "up" your Deserve Level by learning new self-talk strategies.

> **More than six "yes" answers:** You are severely sabotaging yourself. You don't believe you are worthy of achieving the things you desire. To change the situation, you need to update your belief system and change the negative permission from your past. The good news is that you really can change your behavior and your Deserve Level.

▶ **Exercise: Finding Your Self-Sabotage Strategy**

Think of one important goal for this year.

_____

_____

_____

If you were to sabotage this goal, which self-sabotage strategy
or combination of strategies would you use?

_____

_____

_____

Which one of the personal stories do you identify with the
most, and why?

_____

_____

_____

What fear bothers you the most?

_____

_____

_____

3

▼

Beliefs

Creating Ones That Work

"I don't believe it," said Luke Skywalker. "That is why you fail," said Yoda.
—*The Empire Strikes Back*

As you grow up, you're automatically enrolled in an eighteen-year course called "Life Beliefs." This course covers all areas of your existence—religion, career, style, success, whom to marry or not to marry, pleasure, friends, health, and so on. This course is quite complete; we're in class daily and assigned homework by experienced teachers, usually our parents. The material they teach us has a lived-in feel because it's what was taught to them as children.

We absorb our beliefs from the people with whom we grew up—not always the beliefs they said they had, but the ones they lived. Many times in therapy I hear clients say, "I sound just like my mother!" They're shocked to hear themselves responding in ways similar to their parents—perhaps even saying things they swore they'd never think or say.

Like all of us, you grew up in a family that instructed you in word and deed about what life was to be for you. You were well-schooled in beliefs and expectations for yourself that were generated by others. Whether you knew it or not—and even though you never saw the fine print—you cosigned a cognitive and emotional contract that stated what you were entitled to. This contract covered your future thoughts, decisions, feelings, and values.

As you grew up, the power of this Deserve Covenant continued to assert itself. Your beliefs were reflected in your choice of people to love and be close to, the career you chose to establish, the amount of money you earned, and your level of physical and emotional health.

Reading the Fine Print

Some of your beliefs are positive and some aren't. Maybe you were the person in your family who was supposed to be the success, or maybe you were supposed to try hard and barely make it. Maybe you were programmed to have a wonderful, loving marriage, but not to have a flourishing career. Or maybe you were supposed to have a great career, but never have the relationships you wanted.

Just because you have permission in one area doesn't mean you have it in another. You have separate beliefs in every area of your life—and your beliefs shape your view of the world.

Joan Motley, a physician friend, gave me a charming example of how a belief shapes your worldview. Her two-year-old son had met only his mother's female doctor friends. They went to a picnic with all the doctors from the hospital and he became very excited. He ran up to her and said, "Mommy, Mommy! Men are doctors too!" His whole belief system had shifted.

Why Do Beliefs Exercise So Much Power in Your Life?

There are two reasons why your beliefs are so powerful.

1. **Your energy follows your thought.** Your energy goes where your thinking goes. If you stay with a set of negative beliefs, your energy will follow those thoughts—and consequently you

will create more and more negative energy to support those beliefs.

You've had days when nothing you're doing works. When you grab your briefcase, it falls open and spills everything. Your car won't start. You've misplaced your calendar. Everything you touch seems doomed to fail, and you can barely make it through the day.

You stagger home, just glad to be off the highway, and flop down on the couch. Then you get a call from your best friend, who has just had something wonderful happen and wants to celebrate by taking you to dinner. Suddenly you're charged with new energy.

What happened? You were dead; then your thoughts changed; then your energy responded.

2. Whatever you think about you get more of. You get more of whatever you focus on. If you focus on how angry you are at a friend, you're going to find yourself acting more and more angry.

Because your thoughts direct your energy, and the energy you put into your activities then generates their outcome, you have a perfect self-fulfilling prophecy. You get back what you believe will happen even if you consciously want it *not* to happen. A belief is simply a thought you keep practicing.

This is the basis for the concept of worry. You worry about money, and everything seems to drain your resources. You worry about your health, and every ache seems terminal. On the other hand, you can be excited about a new career or relationship and fantasize about all the positives. As your belief expands, you feel more and more wonderful.

Because your beliefs, both conscious and unconscious, have the power to dictate your experience, you keep creating what you believe to be true. Consequently, you never exceed your own expectations.

Beliefs are like icebergs. What sticks up into conscious awareness comprises only about 10 percent of your total belief system. A full 90 percent of your beliefs remain unconscious to your walking-around self until you go looking for them.

These unrecognized beliefs create your thoughts and direct your energy.

Rob did not consciously believe that all employment was precarious. Nonetheless, he unconsciously had the idea that his job would go away someday—so he created what he feared by setting himself up to be fired.

Without realizing it, Rob was reliving an old family tale. His dad had frequently told him about the Depression and how you might think you have a good job, but it can get pulled out from under you at any time. The only thing you could count on was that a company would never appreciate you; after all, his own company had let him go after twenty years.

This story got repeated over and over again, programming Rob to create a self-fulfilling prophecy. He abandoned his jobs before his jobs had a chance to abandon him. Because his thoughts focused on his fear, he created what he wanted to avoid.

Our assimilated beliefs become so ingrained that our behaviors reflect them in repetitive ways. Toni was often told by her father, "You'd lose your head if it weren't attached." Toni still believes she can't keep track of anything! She misplaces car keys, walks away without her purchases, and generally behaves in a forgetful way. At work, she is organized and efficient, but in her personal life, her childhood beliefs run her life in chaotic circles.

How Do We Get Our Beliefs?

In his book *What to Say When You Talk to Yourself,* Shad Helmstetter gives this example of the amount of negative programming most of us have experienced:

> *During the first eighteen years of our lives, if we grew up in a fairly average, reasonably positive home, we were told NO, or what we could not do, more than 148,000 times. If you were a little more fortunate you may have been told NO only 100,000 times, or 50,000 times—however many, it was considerably more negative programming than any of us needs.*

Helmstetter goes on to say that behavioral research tells us that as much as 77 percent of what we think on a daily basis is negative and works against us. Think about that: *whatever good outcomes you're creating are coming from only 23 percent of your potential positive energy.* All day long the litany in your head is draining your energy system. Imagine what you can accomplish when you tap into some of that wonderful unused energy!

As we grow up we internalize, or adopt, the feelings, actions, and bodily responses of the people around us. Our beliefs are a culmination of all the experiences and messages we received from parents, siblings, church, school, the media, and other sources to which we've been exposed.

Beliefs become engraved on us early in our lives and, if left unchanged, can direct our lives from then on. Some of our beliefs are obviously handed to us directly, while others come from *our interpretations* of what people mean. What parents and others say to us is staggering in its importance to our self-esteem and self-confidence.

This is where your Deserve Level begins to become set, and this setting replicates itself over and over through your life experience. At this early stage Deserve Level is about feeling—or not feeling!—a basic *right* to get what you want or need.

The belief in this basic right is formed by the earliest relationship: with one's mother. If we got "good enough" mothering, we felt nurtured during this crucial early period. When we were hungry, wet, needed attention, or reached out for closeness or warmth, the mother figure was there and responded appropriately.

If a disturbance arose at this time, such as mother becoming ill, depressed, or overworked—perhaps attending to other children in the family—we might have felt deprived. We experience this deprivation on a very primal level. We interpret it to the best of our unsophisticated abilities and morph it into a belief that says, "I must not *deserve*—must not be worthy of—love, warmth, or closeness, because I don't get them when I ask for them."

Small children cannot reason with much complexity, but you can see their beliefs in their behavior. A child whose needs are seldom met becomes increasingly quiet and at some point will simply stop trying. Why keep on asking if no one responds? What's the use? The child gives up, feels defeated, and resents the deprivation.

The resentment plus the interpretation of the deprivation readily blend to form an *early decision*—one that's made from a powerful emotional base but is missing key bits of factual information. From such an early decision we can easily imagine the development of a basic limiting belief such as: "If I have to ask for it, it's not worth getting."

David will not ask his wife, Julie, for what he wants. There is a relentless, unconscious battle going on between the part of him that hopes Julie will "notice" and the part of him that fears she never will. His corollary belief, of course, is: "If she really loved me, she would just know. If I have to ask, it means she doesn't care."

Julie never got a degree in mind reading, and she goes crazy trying to guess what David wants. It's not only an unintentional setup for her, it's a no-win situation for everybody.

And this goes even deeper. The second part of David's belief is: "If I *do* ask her, and *then* she responds, it's only because of obligation and guilt, and I don't want her to give me anything for those reasons." Or perhaps he's cobbled together the slightly more noble version: "I don't want to impose on her if she doesn't want to do it."

A setup? Of course. Intentional? No. David's belief system can acknowledge Julie as caring only when she happens to guess correctly what he wants. His belief about himself—his sense of what he deserves—is very low. As Richard Bach writes in *Illusions*: "Argue for your limitations, and sure enough they're yours."

Conversely, I'm reminded that early decisions can also be made in a positive direction. Art Linkletter told a great story when I was sitting with him on a platform some time back. For several years Art hosted a television program called "House Party" and invited small children to be on his show because he enjoyed their candor. He always asked them, "Tell me what your mother told you not to say"—and they did!

He once interviewed a precocious little girl named Krista, who was obviously starting out in life with a belief system that will serve her very well. Art asked Krista, "How were you selected to be on my show?" She replied, "I'm the smartest kid in my class." Art said, "That's very good. Did your teacher tell you that?" Krista said, "No, I noticed it *myself!*"

Life is meant to be full and abundant. There's enough sunlight, air, hope, and love for everyone. If we feel we have to *earn* them—not

have them as a birthright—this belief truly limits us. Our heritage
of hard work, stoicism, and scarcity limits our beliefs and our ability
to accept that we deserve the best.

Many of us have "reasons" why we can't ever achieve our goals.
These beliefs become the anchor that holds us in place. Here are
some of the most common Deserve Level limiting beliefs.

BELIEF LIMITATIONS	THOUGHTS
"I have enough already."	"I have so much that I shouldn't want more."
"I'm not good enough."	"Everyone else deserves it but not me. I'm not good enough (not smart enough, and so on)."
"I haven't suffered enough."	"I haven't earned it (worked hard enough, been unhappy enough) to deserve better for myself."
"It's too good; I don't deserve it."	"I have too much (love, wealth, health). I'm embarrassed by it, so I give it away."
(write in your limiting belief)	(write in your limiting thought)
(write in your limiting belief)	(write in your limiting thought)
(write in your limiting belief)	(write in your limiting thought)
(write in your limiting belief)	(write in your limiting thought)

A client of mine told me that every time he finds himself in
what could turn out to be a great relationship, he becomes more and
more anxious. He has a belief that no one will be able to love him in
the long haul, so he refers to himself as a "love sprinter." When his

anxiety turns to worry and the relationship has lasted longer than is congruent with his internal time-comfort zone, he finds all sorts of work-related matters requiring his attention and makes himself unavailable. Until he changes his beliefs, no relationship can work for him.

Another client of mine shared that she felt guilty every time she got a well-earned bonus check. She felt she didn't deserve it because other people worked so much harder. The only way she could be comfortable was to donate all the money to charity. Until she changed her belief, she never allowed herself to keep any of her bonuses.

When I'm counseling people, I often see them placing a great deal of emphasis on what they don't want to have happen or what they don't want to exist. When asked "What *do* you want?" many people can't answer that question. We all know what we don't want; so to clarify our wants let's start with what we *don't* want to experience or have happen, and then reframe it.

Go at this backwards. Think of five things you don't want, for example:

1. I don't want to miss recruiting this person.
2. I don't want to gain weight.
3. I don't want to be in debt.

▶ **Exercise: What You Don't Want**

I don't want:

_____

_____

_____

_____

_____

Look at your negatives and ask yourself what the flip side is. If you wrote: "I don't want a successful career if it means I won't have a good marriage," your negative thought is: "I can't have a happy marriage and be successful. I can have one but not the other." That's the negative belief that has to be changed, or it will sabotage getting what you want.

Now flip the "don'ts" to what you do want, for example:

1. I want to attract the right people.
2. I want to be healthy, trim, and fit.
3. I want to create all the income I need for my lifestyle choices.

The reverse of the negative belief above could be: "I have a successful career and I'm enjoying my time even more with my family." That statement begins to integrate both beliefs into a positive focus on what you want.

▶ **Exercise: What You Do Want**

Take your five negatives and flip them to the positive side of what you want.

I do want:

_____

_____

_____

_____

_____

Now check how you feel after you say or think each of those.

Remember: We are creating our wants all the time: either deliberately, by focusing on and asking for them, or by default—by focusing on the lack of them.

4

▼

Embrace Self-Esteem and Develop Self-Confidence

To be nobody but yourself in a world that tries
its best day and night to make you everyone else, is
to fight the hardest battle anyone can fight and
never stop fighting.

—E. E. Cummings

Self-esteem and self-confidence are often thought of as emotionally synonymous. Many of us use the words interchangeably, but I believe they're very different.

To have a genuine sense of *self-esteem*, you have to believe you're lovable. My mother let me know that she'd love me even if I'd burned the house down. She had a distinct preference that I not do that, but I knew she'd still love me. Her loving was *unconditional*. She loved me for my *being*, my personhood.

I could, and did, spend hours in my room listening to my records and eating Twinkies, being very unproductive, and she still loved me. In unconditional loving there are no "have-to's" or demands that you do something to be loved. You don't have to earn it, it is just given.

Our level of *self-confidence* is based on the knowledge that we can *do* something worthwhile in life. When I was younger, I would get out my red wagon and sell comic books and lemonade. My dad, who was a national sales manager for a large book company, would walk by and say, "That's my girl. You're a chip off the old block."

I got a great deal of praise for producing and performing. It was *conditional* praise. The same was true when I brought home *A*s on my report card. I learned that I could do some things, and my self-confidence slowly grew.

I knew my mother loved me no matter what I did. And she also wanted me to excel and do well, so I felt her support in both areas and understood that they were separate in her mind. She loved me (heightening my self-esteem) and believed in my abilities to achieve (heightening my self-confidence).

With my dad I wasn't so sure. I knew that he'd approve of me if I got good grades or performed well, but I wasn't so sure that he'd love me if I didn't produce. (The truth is, he loved me all the time. I just didn't believe it until later in life.)

This developed into my adult Deserve Level. I felt loved and supported by women for myself as well as for my achievements. But I'd interpreted my dad's conditional approval as having to "dance for Daddy" or else he wouldn't love me, and that belief generalized to having to perform for men to "earn" their love. Of course, that never worked because you can't earn love.

Still, for a number of years, until I learned this and substantially raised my own Deserve Level, I consistently tried to earn men's love. If a man in my life needed something, I took on the burden of making it happen—a new job, more money, whatever. I would go shopping for myself and end up buying him ties and sweaters. I would plan to be with my girlfriends and then, if he called, I would cancel. I was puppy-dog eager to be helpful, loving, and approved of. If I kept producing, if I did enough to prove my worth and loyalty, then surely he would reward me with his love. It never worked.

I would sometimes wake up with my heart racing, feeling a little nauseated, because I wasn't sure the man in my life really loved me. This anxiety was overwhelming, and my desperation was more than apparent. Men have a built-in radar for desperate women and would quickly move away from me.

Finally, all the disappointment and heartbreak got to be too much. After a lot of failed relationships, I entered therapy, started working on building my self-esteem, and learned to stop manipulating men to give me the approval that only I could give myself. Initially, I felt really scared because I truly had believed that if I ever stopped working hard for love, I wouldn't get even the meager amount of love I was receiving.

Gradually I decided to give up dancing for men's approval. I felt tremendous relief: You mean I don't have to try hard to figure out how to make him love me? You mean that's not the answer to my feelings of loneliness or despair? I began a long process of loving myself first, building my self-esteem, and increasing my Deserve Level in relationships.

Self-Esteem and Self-Confidence in Your Life

Confusion between self-esteem and self-confidence creates massive stress in our lives. Because we get them intermingled in our perception, we tend to "scratch the wrong itch," to compensate inappropriately. But we can have high self-esteem and low self-confidence, or vice versa.

Mike is an extremely self-confident salesperson in the computer industry. He is convinced his product is the best and that all potential prospects would buy it if they just knew about it. He knows that he is in control of his sales, his income, and his professional life. He is always the top producer in his company, and his income reflects it. At the same time, Mike isn't happy in his personal life. Try as he will, he has never had a relationship last longer than two years.

While his self-confidence is high, Mike's self-esteem is shaky. Because he feels unsure of himself in his relationships, he tries to make himself feel better by working harder and harder. The more he works and produces, the more his self-confidence increases. Regrettably, that doesn't change his self-esteem.

Self-esteem is *unconditional acknowledgment for your own worth and lovability.* You are acknowledged for *being* a good person. This creates your sense of being worthy of deserving what you want.

Self-confidence is *conditional acknowledgment for your performance*. You are acknowledged for *doing* something well. This creates your belief that you can earn what you want and that you deserve it because you worked for it.

For healthy self-confidence, you must either do something or have reason to believe, based on past performance, that you can do it. You have to make your quota, or put together a great deal, or run a five-minute mile.

Self-confidence is fostered in a child by encouragement for being capable. The father who gives an "attaboy" to his kid for sinking the baskets, the mother who teaches him how to ride his bike and praises his efforts, are helping him build his self-confidence. That pride in accomplishment and capability becomes transferable—if he knows how to rewire a lamp cord, he is likely to tackle another rewiring job with a degree of certainty.

For healthy self-esteem, you need acknowledgment of who you are as a person, that you are loved and lovable just the way you are.

Self-esteem comes from a child's being told he is a terrific kid, whether he is doing something or not. It tells him about his worth as a person. It is not conditional upon his performance.

Self-esteem and self-confidence influence the choices everyone makes. In her autobiography, *My Life So Far*, Jane Fonda talks about how her low self-esteem affected her relationships with men and pushed her into bulimia:

> *In my public life, I am a strong, can-do woman. How is it, then, that behind the closed doors of my most intimate relations, I could voluntarily betray myself? The answer is this: if a woman has become disembodied due to lack of self-worth—I'm not good enough—or abuse, she will neglect her own voice of desire and only hear the man's. This requires compartmentalizing—disconnecting head and heart, body and soul. Overlay her silence with a man's sense of entitlement and inability (or unwillingness) to read his partner's subtle body signals, and you have the makings of a very angry woman, who will stuff her anger for the same reasons she silences her sexual voice.*

Ellen's Story: Overcoming Setbacks and Creating Comebacks

Ellen Terry is a charming, attractive woman with two grown children and five grandchildren. Many years ago she was the wife of a very successful banker and living a lifestyle we would all envy. She divided her time between important charities, tennis, Junior League, and friends.

Ellen never dreamed her world of affluence was beginning to unwind. She was used to being a stay-at-home mom; she never thought she would have to go to work and become the breadwinner for her children. One afternoon, while she was hosting a Junior League meeting in her home, there was a knock on the door. She answered, and the man on her doorstep said, "I've come to repossess your Mercedes."

At first, Ellen thought there had been a mistake. Her disbelief turned to dismay as she learned that no payments had been made on the car loan in months. Shortly after that, she learned her large home in a premier location in Dallas would have to be sold. Thus began a devastating nightmare that included financial ruin, divorce, and a seven-month separation from her two children, who went to live with their grandparents while Ellen tried to figure out what to do to support them as a single parent.

She began by liquidating all her assets in an effort to pay creditors. Her furniture, jewelry, most of her clothes—everything had to go. Even then, she was left still owing more than $100,000 to the IRS.

Ellen Terry had no car, no job, and no apparent workplace skills. She did, however, have a legacy from childhood—a feeling of self-worth given to her by her parents. She'd been told to be a fighter, not a quitter. She says, "My dad, who was all of five feet, five inches and wore size five cowboy boots, always told me the only inches that mattered were the six inches between your two ears, and whether you perceived things positively or negatively. He taught me that perceiving the glass as half full or half empty is up to you."

She pulled herself up to her full four-foot-ten-inch height and started fighting. Ellen had a deep abiding faith, a strong work ethic, a belief in her God-given potential, and the will to overcome any obstacles by viewing them as challenging opportunities.

Her first goal was to get a job, one that would make enough money for her to bring her kids back home. On the advice of friends, she decided to pursue residential real estate. She says many people discouraged her, saying it was not a promising career and that it would probably take six months to a year to make a sale. Undaunted, Ellen enrolled in real estate school, got her license, and tenaciously interviewed real estate companies. Finally she persuaded Coldwell Banker, the largest nationwide real estate company at the time, to give her a chance.

She says, "I felt like the rabbit that was being chased by the fox. When the farmer yelled out, 'Hey rabbit, you gonna make it?' the rabbit hollered back, 'Make it? Man, I *gotta* make it!' "

The day Ellen passed the exam, she called someone she knew who was thinking about buying a home. In less than a week she had found this client the perfect home. Within six weeks she had sold two houses and made approximately $24,000. By the end of her first full year, she was Coldwell Banker's top salesperson in Texas and second in the nation. She repeated this success her second year with the company.

After her second year in the real estate business, she opened a company with two partners. In 1981 she founded her own company, Ellen Terry Realtors, which is known in Dallas as the "Neiman Marcus of residential real estate," representing multimillion-dollar homes in the luxury market. Her firm is one of the fastest-growing boutique offices in Dallas, selling many of the most expensive homes in Dallas's premier locations.

Ellen Terry says, "I believe there are absolutely no restrictions on what you can do except the ones you create in your own mind. Success is a matter of believing in yourself, being committed to excellence in whatever you do, having the highest level of integrity and ethics, and providing your clients with extraordinary service. Success can be yours if you are never afraid to fail, and when you do fall, get up, dust yourself off, and come back for one more round. Never, never, never give up; train your mind to think positively and you will find that success comes to you. Practice the Golden Rule in your business and daily life and it will come back to you tenfold."

High Self-Esteem, Low Self-Confidence

Margaret is an affluent fifty-year-old housewife who has many wonderful, loving relationships. She's at a time in her life when her children are grown, her husband has retired, and she's also retired from her role as mother. She is tired of volunteer work and wants to do something in the marketplace, wants to produce. She has high self-esteem but low self-confidence because she's thinking of entering an area that is new to her. Because she devoted most of her adult life to caring for her family, she doesn't have the experience to reassure herself she'll be able to perform well in the business world.

"I'd love to go into cosmetic sales," she says, "but I'm just terrified. I don't know if I can do it. What if I fall flat on my face? I want to try, but I'm just too scared."

Her self-esteem is fine. It's her self-confidence that she needs to work on.

High Self-Confidence, Low Self-Esteem

Ironically, whether it's self-confidence or self-esteem that we lack, we tend to make up for the deficiency by using the skills we have in the *opposite arena.*

Mike, the salesperson, used his ability to perform and produce when he tried to create good relationships. He would try to razzle-dazzle and charm his partner, trying to "make her love him." Naturally, this didn't work. You can't sell anyone on loving you; you can only be yourself—and either they will or they won't.

People with high self-confidence and low self-esteem tend to be goal-directed and structure their time. This is a good work habit, but when they bring it home, they try to control their mates and run the show. These people often have a great deal of interpersonal difficulty because the skills that work well in one area may not work in the other.

To compensate and remain comfortable, people with high self-confidence and low self-esteem throw themselves into their jobs, then overachieve. They often make work a substitute for having a social life or friends. As long as they're at work, they seem to have it made, but their personal lives are out of balance as they attempt to nurture themselves with destructive outlets like excessive drinking, illegal drugs, or compulsive sexual encounters.

On the other hand, the person with high self-esteem but low self-confidence might trade on his people skills to the detriment of his performance. Sales managers have heard it often: "I'm a nice person, a good guy, and we're friends. I know I don't make my quota, but come on, keep me on board." As a manager, you don't want to fire such people because they really are likable; but the truth is, they just can't produce.

Managers are also familiar with the person who is fabulous as a producer but is a nightmare to work with (high self-confidence and low self-esteem). Joyce is one of those. A top producer in commercial real estate leasing, Joyce can't seem to get along with any manager. She sees all of them as parental figures, and she rebels—refusing their direction, talking back, telling them they don't know what they're talking about.

Joyce also keeps getting fired. Her sales performance is superb, but she's so impossible to deal with that her beleaguered managers—and, indeed, entire organizations—see her as coming up short in their cost-benefit analysis. Joyce sabotages herself and her future because of her low self-esteem.

How Do You Stack Up?

It is crucial to balance your self-confidence and self-esteem. Why? Because you are a whole person, and eventually you will pay a price if you're out of balance.

If you have more self-confidence than self-esteem, you may be nice and charming, but you tend to get addicted to work and use that as a substitute for close relationships. You probably don't have a support system. You get your satisfaction from accomplishing goals.

If you have more self-esteem than self-confidence, you are thoughtful, considerate, and feel good, but you may lack drive. You get excited by having good relationships, even at work, and are less achievement-oriented; you may not want to concentrate on business. You get all your satisfaction from personal relationships.

Where Are You?

Whichever one gets the lower rating—self-esteem or self-confidence—is the crack in the emotional sidewalk that keeps tripping you up. It's the one you think about when you're driving home alone after work. If your love life (self-esteem) is terrible, you'll focus on that. If your sales are off (self-confidence), you'll focus on that. Inside all of us is the need to complete our unfinished business, to bring the two aspects of our lives into balance. Take this self-test to find out how you rate in your own life.

▶ **Exercise: Creating Self-Esteem**

Remember, self-esteem is unconditional acknowledgment for who you are. It's based on *being*.

Are you likable, lovable? Do you have good relationships with others?

Rate your self-esteem on a scale of one to ten, with one being the lowest and ten being the highest: _____

What is self-esteem?

- Self-esteem does not mean seeing yourself as the greatest person in the world.
- It's not the same as being conceited.

- Healthy self-esteem means liking yourself, for the most part, as you are.
- You can have good self-esteem and still have occasional bouts of self-doubt.

Things that create low self-esteem
- Harsh criticism
- Being abused emotionally or physically
- A lack of intimacy in your life
- Not being noticed or recognized
- Long-term ridicule or teasing
- Unfair expectations of perfection from you, by your peers, parents, or relatives

▶ **Ways to create self-esteem**

Answer the following questions and think about the following prompts, affirming yourself and your relatedness to others:

1. List five positive personal attributes.

_____

_____

_____

_____

_____

2. List five good things about the way you look, feel, think, and act.

_____

_____

_____

_____

_____

3. Whom do you love and who loves you back?

_____

_____

_____

4. Become comfortable with yourself. Accept the flaws and move to what's good.

5. Stop comparing yourself to others.

6. Change what you can and learn to accept yourself for who you are.

7. Learn to laugh at anything, especially yourself.

8. Learn to trust others. Choose friends who treat you as well as you treat them.

9. Try to cultivate love and forgiveness in your life and with other people.

10. Focus on giving to someone in need.

▶ **Exercise: Creating Self-Confidence**

Remember, self-confidence is conditional acknowledgment for what you do or how you perform. It's based on _doing_.

Are you competent and capable? Can you get the things you want done?

Rate your self-confidence on a scale of one to ten, with one being the lowest and ten being the highest: _____

Ways to create self-confidence
- Break tasks into smaller steps.
- Acknowledge success after each step, and celebrate.
- Reinforce your overall confidence.

- Master a task that's new for you.
- Take on a challenge and get acknowledgment for completing it.

Things that create low self-confidence
- You don't acknowledge your success.
- You put your achievement down by saying something like, "Oh, I was just lucky" or "It wasn't all that good."
- You take on a task that's too large.
- You create a task that's too difficult.
- You purposely take on tasks that are way over your head, so you are assured of failure.
- You condemn your faults.
- You are a perfectionist.

▶ **Ways to create self-confidence**

Answer the following questions and think about the following prompts:

1. What do you do well?

_____

_____

_____

2. Who can give you praise for doing something well?

_____

_____

_____

5

▼

Permission from Your Past

SOMETIMES A PERSON HAS TO GO BACK, REALLY BACK—
TO HAVE A SENSE, AN UNDERSTANDING OF ALL THAT'S
GONE TO MAKE THEM—BEFORE THEY CAN GO FORWARD.
—Paule Marshall, *The Chosen Place,*
the Timeless People

YOUR HISTORY IS written deeply into your psyche. Your past goes with you and haunts you if it's unresolved. All of us grew up in families that gave or withheld permission for success—sometimes both at once. Some of us came from families that cheered us on at whatever we wanted to achieve. Others came from families that were more cautious, perhaps a little scared for us, so their admonitions held us back. Some of us came from dysfunctional families that taught us by word and deed what it was to self-destruct.

Within this culture men and women are often told—directly or indirectly—that they are limited to specific roles. If you wanted to do something outside these specified boundaries, you may not have received permission to do it, and you then had to struggle with giving yourself permission.

Your *programs for living*—what you heard about yourself, or what your parents did with their lives: the models they showed you—are part of your permission system.

You inherited your permission system from all the stories, myths, and statements that your family or important mentors made about you. You were told about your abilities, in word and in behavior, by the people closest to you. Your personal beliefs about yourself are scripted into your permission system; it, in turn, follows you and directs your life's course.

Maybe you're a people person, an extrovert "just like Dad." Dad happens to be a top-ranked insurance salesman, so naturally you'd be good in sales.

Sometimes permission comes from important people other than your parents. Jim's leadership abilities, for example, were anchored into his unconscious by a strong relationship with his parish priest. Jim was trained in life lessons by the Jesuits' beliefs in service and sacrifice for others. He became the youth fellowship president of his church club. One afternoon his mentor came up to him, took hold of his arm, and said, "You will be a very important man one day. You are a leader of men." This permission went right through to Jim's unconscious and became a powerful psychological imprint. He grew up to become a recognized leader in the broadcasting field and a highly active community leader.

Some of us are *lacking permission* from our past. When we go after something of value to us, we run into blocks and sabotage ourselves because deep inside we don't believe we can have it or that we have a right to it. This can create enormous conflict within us.

Sally had spent thousands of dollars on therapy and still couldn't lose the weight she said she wanted to lose. She did an exercise in my seminar in which she closed her eyes and told her mother what she wanted (to lose fifty pounds), then clearly heard her mother say, "Don't fool with diets, they never work anyway." No wonder her weight-loss attempts never lasted.

Maybe you got *mixed permission*. From one parent you may have heard, "You can't do that!" and from the other, "That's great, kid, you can do it!" When you move toward a new goal that will push you beyond your comfort zone, you get two messages in your head. Guess what? Your action becomes ambivalent, and you take one step forward and one step back, depending upon which permission is more in the forefront at that moment.

Many people got mixed permission from the same parent. One time you'd hear one thing, and another time another. You'll need to sort out which "voice" has your attention most of the time.

Sometimes a parent said one thing and acted out another—the old "Do what I say, not what I do" maxim—which means you may have learned to do this as well. Ever hear yourself say, "I know I shouldn't do this, but . . . "?

Your parents did the best job they could and loved you the best way they knew how. Sometimes what you heard was not what they actually said; instead it was your *interpretation* of what they said, based on a particular set of perceptions you had at the time.

Your parents may now have tremendous support for you without you realizing it. The limitations they placed on you when you were small may have long since disappeared in their minds—but not in yours.

Your permission system was implanted by age five. If it hasn't been updated, the permissions—or lack of them—remain the same. This means that you're living your life based on permission you were or were not given when you were five!

If you believed then that you were shy and retiring, and therefore wouldn't have good relationships, you will live this out your whole life until you change that early programming.

Think about what your family said about relationships. Does everyone in your family stay happily married, or is divorce the accepted way? Is your father the boss, or your mother the negative one? What kind of romantic partner are you attracted to? Does this person remind you of a parent?

The challenge is for you to give yourself *new adult permission* to believe you can have what you want or to lead a different life. You can find alternative sources within yourself and from other people for the permission you don't currently have.

Money is another powerful issue in our permission system. How did your parents handle money? Visualize yourself asking your parents for money: what do they say? How do they feel about people who have money and people who lack it? What is money to be used for—fun, savings, or just to squeak by? How much is enough? Do they believe that *you* could make money?

Brittany Bursts Through Her Sabotage

Brittany is an entrepreneur who built her business by her own efforts. Every year she made $60,000 while other people who had similar businesses were easily making $80,000 to $100,000. As soon as she got close to the $60,000 figure, she slowed down and stopped producing. Brittany knew she was settling for less than she could achieve, but she didn't know why.

As we talked together, we found out that her mom had died when she was young and her father had never made more than $60,000. She had an unconscious fear about doing better than he did. Her fear was that if she made more money than he did, she might lose his love—and the love was more important to her than the money.

As we talked, I asked her, "Will he not love you at $61,500?" She laughed and decided to find out. She picked up the phone, called him, and said, "Dad, I want to make more money. Will you love me if I make more money than you do?"

Her father replied, "Honey, I'm going to love you no matter how much money you make. Go ahead and make $200,000 and you can buy me a steak dinner to celebrate."

Brittany got her new permission not to settle for less than she deserved and made $150,000 the next year. I told her that if I'd had a higher Deserve Level, I'd have charged her a commission, not a flat fee!

And how about permission for health? Are you in a "heart-attack family"? What are your family's stories about longevity and personal health? At what age do you expect to get ill, or do you expect to stay healthy until you die?

Few people will find it productive to actually go back to their parents to ask which permissions they didn't get so many years ago. You'll discover by your behavior what permissions you did and didn't get. There's no magic in this: just look at what you're doing and at your outcomes, and from there you'll be able to find the trail back to the origins of your dilemma.

Once you know what your internal permission system has not been allowing you to have, you can change it. Until then, you'll find yourself passing the buck and blaming outside factors:

- "The economy is lousy, no wonder I can't get ahead!"
- "I work and work and never make good money."
- "There are no good single men/women left."
- "It's always office politics."
- "Be happy with what you have, don't be selfish."
- "It's all my partner's fault."

You have not only the power to find out how you're blocked, but also the power to change it. Isn't that a lot better than the powerless position brought about by thinking life is "doing it" to you?

Actress Mariette Hartley has appeared in dozens of television shows, including "Peyton Place," "Dr. Kildare," "The Twilight Zone," "The Love Boat," and "Law and Order." She also held the position of news anchor on the CBS "Morning Show." She works tirelessly with recovery groups and is a champion for people who have been abused as well as people struggling with addictions. She has personally experienced both and is living testimony that you can overcome your history:

> *Even the wonderful things in my growing up had an edge of negativity of judgment. And the big voice in my head wasn't my dad's. He was mushy and adored me—there was that whole wonderful, unspoken feeling that he and I got each other creatively. It was my mother's, without understanding. So often those people who don't give us what we need, it's from their limitation rather than ours. But when you're the fish in this tank asking for food or whatever growing up, you don't know that. . . . How do you walk away from this kind of family mythology, when that's what you know? Instead, you begin to abuse yourself and do shameful things because you can't win. It's taken me years to uncover these scars.*
>
> *I got into therapy and was able to make the emotional break from my mother, which was extraordinarily difficult because there was total enmeshment. Now they call it* codependency. *It was a very difficult relationship to pull myself away from. I finally said, "This is ridiculous. What's the point?" Even though the alcohol had kind of freed me and released me. That's what happens to women alcoholics.*

Mariette Hartley clearly came to see that these old, powerful messages from the past needed to be dramatically rescripted. Her determination to do that has enabled her to be a very effective example of the power to change.

Career Permission

As Wanda Wolfe so profoundly states in a personal letter she sent me:

When I heard you speak at our conference you talked about getting permission from our past. This is when I realized what was holding me back. It was me*!*

I came from a very poor family that dealt with hardship as the way of life. My father was a coal miner with a quick right hand for discipline and a third-grade education. He only gave criticism, never love or encouragement. My mother had a seventh-grade education and didn't think anyone needed more than that. I was afraid to be smarter than they were. I heard their voices from my childhood saying: "Don't be such a smart aleck! Keep your big mouth shut!" So I did. I was afraid to ask questions or voice my opinion about anything. My mom's favorite saying when asked for anything we couldn't afford—which was almost everything: "Don't ask for things you can't have. That's stupid."

I knew I had to get out of my own way if I was to become successful. So I did as you suggested and got a picture of my parents and started talking to them honestly for the first time. I certainly couldn't do that when they were alive. It was quite difficult at first, but I continued talking to them. I even forgave them.

You talked about people who were afraid to earn more money than their parents, but got permission to do so. Ah! I knew that I had already earned more than both my parents combined, but I didn't want to be a "smart aleck"—so I was holding myself back. Then I asked for their permission. Guess what? It was given!

I'm still doing the self-talk and affirmations after two years. I have raised my self-esteem and have confidence in myself that I never had. I deserve it!

The Past Is Prologue

Feelings and thoughts from our past become imprinted on our future selves. If we don't like what we're achieving, we have to change it.

One of my permission issues was about my career and money. I grew up in a traditional family with Dad as the breadwinner and Mom working part-time as a teacher. As I developed my speaking career, I wanted to be successful; I wanted to make more money than I had as a therapist. When I had those dialogues with my parents (inside my head, not in person), I heard my mother say, "You can do anything you decide, honey. You've always been good at whatever you decided to do." My dad, on the other hand, was more reticent and withholding of support. He said, "I don't think you can be that successful—you're a woman, and that's a man's business."

Because I had *mixed permission* for success, I had a stop-and-start career. I was ambivalent, so I'd take two steps forward and one back. I got successful only when I resolved that ambivalence by focusing my thoughts on something new. Instead of focusing on what my father said, I created a new affirmation: "I love and honor my father, *and* I choose to create a successful speaking career."

This is a very important psychological point: regardless of the degree to which our childhood was loving, extremely challenging, or somewhere in between, all of us feel a kind of loyalty to the people who raised us. This loyalty factor sometimes extends to living the life *they* imagined for us rather than the one *we* want. In all my work with people's deserve issues, I have found that many of us are trying to show our love and loyalty—or perhaps gain acceptance at last—by living out our parents' beliefs, not ours.

We can love our parents *and* live the lives we want and deserve to. We can love them and still have more for ourselves. As one of my clients said to me, "Are you future-focused or past-possessed?"

▶ **Exercise: Parental Permission**

Think of something you want for yourself. It can be anything—more money, a better love life, a new car, anything.

Now fantasize that you're talking with your father; tell him what you want for yourself. What is his response? How does he look? What is he saying? Is he supportive, disbelieving, or critical?

Now pretend you're talking with your mother. What is her response? Look at her face. Is she with you or not? What does she say about what you want?

Review your parents' different responses. Whom do you feel supported by? Do you have permission to get what you want?

What are the messages you got from your parents? You may still be treating yourself the same way you were treated as a child. If you didn't like any of the responses you got, check to be sure that *you* aren't still giving yourself these same messages.

Give yourself a few minutes to think about all this. Jot down what permissions you do or do not have, and star the ones you want to have more of.

Permissions from My Past

FROM MY MOTHER

Positive Permissions

Career: _____

_____

Love: _____

_____

Health: _____

_____

Finances: _____

_____

Negative Permissions

Career: _____

_____

Love: _____

_____

Health: _____

_____

Finances: _____

_____

FROM MY FATHER

Positive Permissions

Career: _____

_____

Love: _____

_____

Health: _____

_____

Finances: _____

_____

Negative Permissions

Career: _____

_____

Love: _____

_____

Health: _____

_____

Finances: _____

_____

FROM SPOUSE OR PARTNER

Positive Permissions

Career: _____

_____

Love: _____

_____

Health: _____

_____

Finances: _____

_____

Negative Permissions

Career: _____

_____

Love: _____

_____

Health: _____

_____

Finances: _____

_____

Now that you understand the unconscious power of permission from your past, you are ready to move into a powerful new phase: deciding what you really want. Not what others wanted for you, not what you are "supposed to" want, but what *you* truly want.

You can't change the statements important people made to you many years ago, but you can change your repetitive reactivation and reinforcement of those permissions. You can change the internalized parents' voices to a message that you want now. You *don't* need *them* to change. You can change your repetition of the old message.

▶ **Exercise: New Permissions (you fill in the blank)**

An example would be: "I love and honor my parents and I choose

_____

_____."

I choose to create all the _____

_____ I want.

(For more detail on affirmations and new permissions, see Chapter 12: Self-Talk.)

PART II

▼

Self-Sabotage

Why Does This Keep
Happening to Me?

6

▽

I Can Get It, but I Can't Keep It

The Throwing-It-Away Sabotage Strategy

THE GREATER DANGER FOR MOST OF US IS NOT THAT OUR
AIM IS TOO HIGH AND WE MISS IT, BUT THAT IT IS TOO
LOW AND WE REACH IT.

—Michelangelo

SELF-SABOTAGE CAN BE a remarkably subtle phenomenon. You can be doing it repeatedly and almost systematically throughout your life, yet continue to be amazed that certain things "keep happening" to you. The chapters in Part II will introduce you to five primary sabotage strategies so that you can start to see how you get in your own way. If you catch yourself saying, "Aha, that's it, that's me!" you can begin the process of change.

Self-sabotage is not as simple as having low self-esteem or receiving negative messages from our parents. For each of us, it's a complex pattern woven from our experiences, what was said and our interpretation of what was said, and the early-life decisions we made as a result. We tend to follow this pattern, acting and reacting in terms of it, until we learn there are other options. And there always are.

We're born into a family whose members think, speak, and act in certain ways. In our early years, no matter how functional or dysfunctional those ways actually are, they're immediately "normal" to us—they're simply how things are done, how life is to be lived. Even when behavior in the family is outrageous and abnormal, our survival instinct normalizes it because we have nothing as yet with which to compare it.

We also have nowhere else to go. If Mom repeatedly calls me selfish, or Dad relentlessly reminds me that "people in this family just aren't college material," or Grandpa believes "all short people are clumsy," it must be true because they're the grown-ups, and surely they know what they're talking about. And surely they're preparing us for the real world.

When we're out on our own, that "normal" way of perceiving ourselves and others becomes a "normal" way of thinking and behaving and relating to the world. "Well, I just know that nothing I do will work anyway [resignation], so why should I try?" Or, "I'm so used to being handed whatever is left over [settling for less], it's really okay if that's all there is." Or, "You know, it's pretty clear that everyone's doing me in, and I don't really have any power over my life here [denial]."

Because the pattern is so familiar, we don't see it. It's like walking into a room every day and not noticing the furniture. A client once told me, "I really don't see what I have to do with all this—these things just happen to me." It looks like fate.

In my work, however, I've found that we all do have a sneaking suspicion as to how we're limiting ourselves. In my seminars, I regularly ask, "If you were to sabotage your goals in the next year, how would you do it?" People always smile—and rather spontaneously say, "Well, I would . . . "

Your particular form of self-sabotage can be as unique as your own fingerprint, and there are limitless ways in which all of us can sell ourselves short. In my experience, though, there are five major categories which, when understood, will help alert you to this destructive tendency.

Once you have recognized one or more of your particular sabotage strategies (settling-for-less sabotage, resignation sabotage, denial sabotage, throwing-it-away sabotage, or fatal-flaw sabotage), you can go on to Part III to discover all your options for change. Take advantage of those options, and you'll have daily evidence that not only do you deserve more, but you can most certainly have it.

You've worked hard to reach a certain level of success in your health or relationships or career. Why can't you relax and enjoy your success? Why do you throw away something you've worked hard to achieve?

One of the scariest statistics I've read about *throwing-it-away sabotage* comes from the National Football League: within two years of leaving the NFL, 78 percent of all football players are bankrupt, divorced, or unemployed. Many are all three. What happened to these superstars?

The answer to that question is the same for everyone: when we don't truly believe we deserve success, we have to get rid of it—we feel compelled to throw it away in order to return to psychic equilibrium.

The sabotage strategy of throwing it away is created when people exceed their Deserve Level limits. The new reality (a better body, more money, or a wonderful relationship) takes us out of our comfort zone. We now have a difficult choice to make: we can raise our Deserve Level and celebrate that new reality, or we can throw it away and feel an odd kind of relief. People who have a *post-achievement sabotage strategy* reach their goals but feel too uncomfortable with success, so they unconsciously throw it away.

In other words, we too often choose (without seeing *how* we're choosing) to keep ourselves within our Deserve Level limits, our comfort zone, by giving away what we've truly wanted and worked hard to achieve. Once we realize the origin of our problems and de-power our inner demons, we can turn sabotage to success.

Oprah: The Queen of Talk Values Personal Development

Oprah's odyssey with weight has been a long, dramatic, and very public one. Her belief in sharing the ups and downs of personal development has moved her to talk about her struggles with her millions of loyal fans for two decades now.

Her issues in this area began in her childhood. Food became her emotional teddy bear, nurturing her through difficult times growing up. Cookies never abandon you; cake never talks back; and in a world of uncertainty, chocolate is a constant, loving companion.

At her heaviest, the five-foot-six-and-a-half-inch Winfrey weighed 237 pounds. When she won a Daytime Emmy in 1992 and was at her heaviest, she was quoted in *People* magazine as saying, "I felt so much like a loser."

In her outer life she was honored, loved, and revered for her TV show; and in her inner life she felt miserable. She would reach her goal weight, then sabotage herself by putting the weight back on. This yo-yo behavior also had a definite impact on her health.

But Oprah is a great example of a celebrity turnaround. She took charge of her weight issue and committed to a healthy lifestyle. As she said, "After many years of my weight going up and down, I realized that the commitment to do well and to be well is a lifetime of choice that you make daily."

Her struggle has simultaneously epitomized and highlighted our tremendous national problem. Every medical report affirms that we're becoming an "overweight nation," riddled with obesity-related diseases ranging from childhood diabetes to adult cardiac problems. Oprah has turned her odyssey with weight into a health and diet initiative for thousands of fans. She resolved her dysfunctional past of overeating and using food as love by giving herself new permission to empower herself and women everywhere to make better choices and to stop using food as a substitute for other emotional needs.

Janet Throws Them Out

Janet is a tall redhead—articulate, driven, and a very successful account executive. She's very attractive to everyone she meets because she listens and genuinely cares about her relationships. She was on her third marriage when she came to see me about her relationship sabotages. Janet recognized that she had somehow participated in the two prior breakups and saw herself on her way to destroying this third marriage. She also recognized that this man was too good to throw away.

She described a pattern; she would have a great time dating and getting to know the man in her life, but when she turned him into a husband, her whole personality would change. She would criticize and scrutinize his every decision, career move, and attitude. Eventually she demoralized her spouses so completely that they left. She passively, gradually "threw them away" by making them terribly uncomfortable.

Janet had witnessed many divorces in her immediate and extended family and seemed to believe there was no way for her to be an exception to this "rule." Therefore, since no committed relationship was likely to last, it was unconsciously less painful to take charge and get rid of the marriage before it got rid of her.

As we talked and Janet committed to looking at her patterns in more depth, she came to understand that this negative family script had existed for more than two generations. As a result, she decided she didn't have to live that script and could, in fact, rewrite it. She brought her husband in for three sessions, took responsibility for the negative way she'd been dealing with him, and apologized. She acknowledged that if he had been treating her the way she was treating him, she'd have left the marriage long ago. Janet vowed to correct her behavior toward him, and she did. They've now been married for more than ten years.

Kiss the Money Good-Bye

Bob is a very charming and gifted salesman. He loves his product, loves his business, and is always at the top of the sales rankings in his company. One year, his company instigated a promotional sales bonus campaign. Whoever sold the most in the next twelve-month period would receive a $25,000 check. Bob was inspired; he wanted that bonus, and he worked really hard to earn it.

On the day of the announcement, he arrived in his best suit and claimed the prize. But within a week he'd gambled it away! He didn't believe he deserved such a big check—"it just felt strange"—and was comfortable again only when he had gotten rid of it.

Bob had come from a middle-class family that wanted him to do well but had emphasized that "you get only what you work for." Up until the time of this bonus, he'd worked extremely hard and was very comfortable with all his success. Once he saw the numbers on the actual check, though, he was thrown into a Deserve Dilemma. He'd worked extra hard, but couldn't reconcile for himself that he'd worked an extra $25,000 worth. No one in his family had ever been handed a lump sum that large, and it so exceeded his Deserve Level boundaries that he literally could not bear the anxiety that came with keeping it. So he "had to" throw it away.

He Threw Away the Presidency

Richard Nixon will go down in history as one of the most complex and conflicted men in public life. He's one of the most obvious examples of the throwing-it-away sabotage strategy.

Nixon's political career had many ups and downs. In 1952 Dwight Eisenhower chose him as his vice-presidential candidate. He held that office for eight years, lost the 1960 presidential election to John F. Kennedy, regrouped, and came back to win in 1968 against Hubert Humphrey in one of the closest elections in U.S. history.

Nixon finally had what he'd been wanting for twenty years: the presidency! After years of turmoil with the Vietnam War in his first term, he was nonetheless reelected by a landslide in 1972. Then he risked his reputation and entire political future by agreeing to the Watergate break-in and subsequently lying about his complicity.

Watergate is the term used to describe a series of political scandals between 1972 and 1974. The word specifically refers to the Watergate Hotel in Washington, D.C., and the burglary of the Democratic National Committee offices by people working for Nixon. When confronted, Nixon lied and tried to cover up his involvement. What kind of fear or paranoia would allow a president to stoop to this kind of criminal behavior when he'd already won the election?

The aftermath of Watergate would change American politics forever. The discovery of this corruption and cover-up—combined with the resignation of Richard Nixon in August 1974—brought forth not only a new level of media scrutiny of our leaders, but a massive disillusionment with them as well. This is a case of one person's self-sabotage changing the lives of millions of people.

Nixon was acting out of his own fear and paranoia when he authorized an illegal act. This authorization reflected a "victim stance" and an ongoing fear-based belief that everyone was out to get him. Fear pushed the most public figure in the world to do something outside the law, thus setting up his throwing-it-away self-sabotage. Following an earlier loss he had famously said, "You won't have Nixon to kick around anymore." He made sure of that once and for all with the Watergate fiasco.

How Big Winners Throw It Away

In various surveys on happiness, people are asked, "What would make you happier?" The overwhelmingly common answer is "more money"—and the larger the check, the better. Many of us have bought a lottery ticket and dreamed of the life we'd surely lead once those millions of dollars were in the bank. However, the reality that actually accompanies receipt of the large inheritance, the long-awaited financial settlement, or the lottery check can be quite different from what anyone expected.

Research shows that roughly one-third of lottery winners find themselves in serious financial trouble—or bankrupt—within five years of turning in their lucky numbers. Here are some real-life stories of throwing it away, from "Eight Lottery Winners Who Lost Their Millions" in *MSN Money*:

> *Evelyn Adams says, "Winning the lottery isn't always what it's cracked up to be." Adams won the New Jersey lottery not just once, but twice (in 1985 and 1986), to the tune of $5.4 million. Today, the money is all gone and Adams lives in a trailer.*

"I won the American dream, but I lost it too. It was a very hard fall. It's called rock bottom," says Adams. "Everybody wanted my money. Everybody had their hand out. I never learned one simple word in the English language—'No.' I wish I had the chance to do it all over again. I'd be much smarter about it now," says Adams, who also lost money at the slot machines in Atlantic City.

William Post won $16.2 million in the Pennsylvania lottery in 1988 but now lives on Social Security. "I wish it never happened. It was totally a nightmare," says Post.

A former girlfriend successfully sued him for a share of his winnings, and it wasn't his only lawsuit. A brother was arrested for hiring a hit man to kill him, hoping to inherit a share of the winnings. Other siblings pestered him until he agreed to invest in a car business and a restaurant in Sarasota, Florida—two ventures that brought no money back and further strained his relationship with his siblings.

Post even spent time in jail for firing a gun over the head of a bill collector. Within a year, he was $1 million in debt. He admitted he was both careless and foolish, trying to please his family. He eventually declared bankruptcy, and now lives quietly on $450 a month and food stamps.

William Hurt of Lansing, Michigan, won $3.1 million in 1989. Two years later he was broke and charged with murder. His lawyer says Hurt spent his fortune on a divorce and crack cocaine.

Missourian Janite Lee won $18 million in 1993. Lee was generous to a variety of causes, giving to politics, education, and the community. According to published reports, eight years after winning, Lee had filed for bankruptcy and had only $700 left in two bank accounts and no cash on hand.

Victoria Zell, who shared an $11 million Powerball jackpot with her husband in 2001, is serving time in a Minnesota prison, and her money is gone. Zell was convicted in March 2005 for a drug and alcohol-induced collision that killed one person and paralyzed another.

Two years after winning a $31 million Texas lottery in 1997, Billie Bob Harrell Jr. committed suicide. He had bought cars and real estate and had given money to his family, church, and friends.

After his death it was not clear whether there was money left for estate taxes.

"For many people, sudden money can cause disaster," says Susan Bradley, a certified financial planner in Palm Beach, Florida, and founder of the Sudden Money Institute, a resource center for new-money recipients and their advisors.

"In our culture, there is a widely held belief that money solves problems. People think if they had more money, their troubles would be over. When a family receives sudden money, they frequently learn that money can cause as many problems as it solves," she says.

There are many emotional issues tied up in money. Although these lottery winners probably didn't examine their Deserve Level issues, I think subconsciously their windfalls became too much for them to handle. Their emotional equilibrium only returned when they threw the money away. But there are other winners who have learned to embrace the wonderful gift of a big prize by raising their Deserve Level to handle it.

You've read the examples in every area of life—health, career, money, and relationships. How do they apply to you? Are you sabotaging your success by throwing it away? Do you reach goals and then get rid of the success as fast as possible?

The first step in any personal change is awareness. You can stop the throwing-it-away sabotage, but you first need to admit that's what you are doing.

▶ Exercise: The Throwing-It-Away Sabotage Strategy

Ask yourself these questions:

1. What have I achieved and felt uncomfortable with?

_____

_____

_____

_____

2. What achievements have I thrown away?

_____

_____

_____

3. Did I unconsciously believe that I did not deserve the achievement?

_____

_____

_____

_____

7

Pass Me the Leftovers

The Settling-for-Less Sabotage Strategy

WE HAVE MET THE ENEMY AND HE IS US.
—Walter Kelly, *Pogo*

THE *SETTLING-FOR-LESS SABOTAGE strategy* can be seen whenever people get within sight of their goals and then do something to self-destruct beforehand. They're always the bridesmaids but never the brides. They go into the store of life to buy a Mercedes and come out with a Chevy. They're all set to check in at the Ritz-Carlton but somehow end up at a Comfort Inn. They try on Prada and end up buying at Kmart.

In self-sabotage we each have a different sense of timing around when we choose (again, mostly unconsciously) to wreck our dreams. Many people have a *pre-achievement sabotage strategy*, which means they get right up to the last mile and then make sure they don't go over the finish line. They live in an "almost" script. They almost win the tournament or the prize, but at the last moment choose defeat instead of victory. As they get close to a goal, they freeze, become

Bambi in the headlights, and settle for less than what they really want.

Some of the beliefs that make up this sabotage strategy are "I want it, but I don't really deserve it, so it's okay if I settle for less," or "I want it, but I'm scared of what having it will mean, so maybe it's best I quit while I'm ahead." I've worked with many people who simply freeze when they're right at the brink of a personal achievement, a loving relationship, or career success.

Why do we settle for less?

Why do we say we're going to lose thirty pounds, lose only five, and then quit?

Why do we start a wonderful new relationship, then find every flaw that person has and walk away?

Why do we decide on the career position we want and never apply for it?

Sometimes our settling has to do with an overwhelming feeling that "this is too much." We feel guilty, embarrassed, even ashamed of our success, so we put the brakes on. "What will my friends think if I buy a big, new house? How will my family feel about me?" This fear of success isn't really a fear of what we can have—it's a fear about the emotional price we will have to pay for it.

Hart Races to Self-Sabotage

Gary Hart's race for the presidency is a clear lesson in *settling for less*.

In 1988 Gary Hart was the front-runner in the race for the Democratic nomination until he sabotaged his career. He had worked and campaigned for many years to reach that powerful position and was within sight of securing it when he blew it all apart in one afternoon.

He'd been questioned by the press more than once about his alleged womanizing, so he dared them to "put a tail on" him and check it out for themselves. The next weekend he was photographed on the appropriately named boat *Monkey Business* with model Donna Rice on his lap. That photo ended his presidential career.

The married Democratic senator told the media that she just dropped into his lap. In turn, the American public dropped him.

What was he thinking? First, by daring the media to tail him, and then within days of that, by cavorting with Donna Rice on a boat! This was clearly a man with internal conflicts regarding his desire and his capacity to be president. His fears and negative beliefs won, and he lost his chance to be a presidential candidate. He had sabotaged himself before he even got the nomination, and he ended up settling for so much less than he could have had.

Mom Has Settled for Less for a Long Time

Cathy, a client of mine, told me a poignant story about her mother. Just after moving into her first new apartment, Cathy invited her mother to come for dinner—in fact, her mom's favorite dinner. Cathy spent all day cleaning the house and readying the special meal. As she watched her mother just pick at the food, Cathy asked, "What's the matter? I fixed your favorite meal—chicken backs!"

Her mom said, "Oh, I never really liked chicken backs. I only ate them because that's all that was left after you kids got the white meat." Cathy's mom had grown up in a home and a culture that never listened to what she liked or wanted. She had lived a lifetime of settling for less, never asking for what she desired.

Julie Learns to "Lean Forward"

Here's a letter I received from one of my clients, Julie Sharla:

I run my own direct-selling business, and my income is dependent on what I do and how I help my people be successful. My self-sabotage was that I settled for less than what I really wanted. I wanted to be more successful, but I kept hearing my mother's voice in my head saying, "You're so lucky to be doing as well as you are. You have food on your table and a car. Just be happy where you are."

Her experiences as an orphan in the Depression created her low Deserve Level and low self-esteem. I don't blame her, as she did the best with what she had. However, I wanted more, and I felt a bit guilty. I was like the two Olympic sprinters that are going neck-and-neck to the finish. One sprinter leans forward, and one pulls up. I pull up!

I had a dream that gave me some clarity: I was driving to an appointment and was on time. I could see the light of my destination, but for no reason at all I pulled over and stopped. I turned off the engine, then started to panic: "Why?" I tried to start the car, but it wouldn't turn over. All of a sudden a woman in a black dress came to the side of the car, reached over, and started the engine. The person turning the key was me trying to get me started again.

Pat, your coaching and insight has made a dramatic difference in my business and my life. I learned to create new positive affirmations instead of listening to the old, limiting ones. I changed my self-talk, and that changed my business.

Within six months of working with you I had three new business builders, got special recognition for recruiting and production, and earned my first car from the company. You truly helped me to understand myself and get inside my own head.

Right now I'm doing great, but I realize that, when things are going well, we sometimes quit doing the things that got us there. It's important to keep up that new behavior, listen to those new affirmations, and stay focused on deserving more.

Greg Norman "Almost" Wins

The golf pro Greg Norman is someone we can all relate to: he gets right up to the finish line and chokes. He's a fascinating example because his talent is obvious, and it's quite clear he can win, yet in the last moments he snatches defeat from the jaws of victory. This pattern of almost winning happens to him time and time again. Even the best among us can have a bad day, and everyone can feel under tremendous pressure to succeed, but Norman's settling-for-less sabotage is repetitive in a way that rivets our attention.

Romance: Don't Settle, Keep the Hope Alive

Over 50 percent of marriages end in divorce. In a personal letter to me from a woman I'll call Sharon, we find someone who learned important lessons about settling:

> *I have known divorce. Twice. I know that feeling of mind-numbing grief, of despair, of hopelessness and failure. I know that no one ever gets married thinking it will someday end in divorce.*
>
> *Both my divorces were awful. I didn't get any better at it after the first time. It's not something for which you acquire a talent. Each marriage offered its own gifts, and the significant relationships in my life have offered doorways into my soul, have opened up part of me that might have otherwise remained dormant. But those two divorces offered me opportunities to discover how I consistently sabotaged myself out of my own power as a woman. As had been the case with other men in my life, both these men were impressive, charismatic, powerful in the world, and I consistently hid my own light in the shadow of theirs. When I recognized how I'd settled for so much less than I deserved—because I believed what I had was the best I deserved—it was quite sobering. I hadn't realized I was the one making the choice; I was deciding what level of happiness to give myself.*
>
> *I finally gave up hope of ever finding a partner who would offer me the kind of love I was willing to offer him. I wanted so much to have a romantic partner, to be part of a team, but I'd reached a point where I knew that I'd never again settle for less than I was willing to give. . . .*
>
> *When I met Roger, I knew that all my old behaviors were over. I was no longer settling—indeed, quite the opposite. He offered me more than, in my old sense of myself, I'd ever thought possible—only now I was quite ready to receive it. I had the dream come true.*
>
> *Today I'm filled with a rush of gratitude as I remember both the pain and the gifts of those marriages. I breathe deeply and send a message of forgiveness to both former husbands—and to myself. Forgiveness is the greatest healer and is surely one of the cornerstones of healing myself of self-sabotage once and for all.*

Are You Settling for Too Little?

Settling for less can be a sly process because it sometimes masquerades as humility or simply letting others succeed before you do—or in place of you. There's a goodness and an ennobling quality about passing up the bigger piece of the pie. That's the rationalization people use when they have divided their Deserve Levels into smaller amounts. They say, "Why would I want more? Who am I to strive? After all, isn't that just a bit greedy?"

There's a discounting and belittling in those words. You want more because that's what you want! You don't have to justify it or settle for too little. And has it ever occurred to you that the world would benefit greatly by having all of us able to function at our full capacities, with full access to all the resources we need?

I worked with a lawyer who spent seventy-hour weeks trying hard to make partner in her firm. After years of proving herself, she was told that she wouldn't ever be made a partner and that was that. That announcement shook her to her core, but instead of finding a firm that appreciated her, she settled by telling herself, "I'm helping the poor through my pro bono work, and that's enough." She settled for less until her anger erupted into an ulcer and depression, and she made a new decision not to settle anymore. She's now a partner in a smaller firm that appreciates her talents—and she can still do the pro bono work of her choice.

This sabotage strategy of settling for less is a major psychological factor behind what's called "midlife crisis." In midlife all of us have a period of reassessment in which we think about what we may be missing because of the choices we've made. We wonder, "Did I settle too soon?"

If you're married, you think about being single. If you're single, you may want to be married.

If you're working, you want to quit. If you've quit, you want to work.

If you have kids, you want them to be gone. If you don't have them, you want them.

The eternal question is: "Am I living the life I want, or have I settled for too little?" If any of these thoughts go through your mind, take this quiz:

▶ **Exercise: The Settling-for-Less Sabotage Strategy**

1. When I get close to my goal, I slow down or stop doing what has made me successful.

   YES   NO

2. I don't feel I deserve more, I have enough already. I should be happy with what I've got.

   YES   NO

3. Everyone else deserves success more than I do. By comparison, I don't feel I'm as good as they are.

   YES   NO

4. I feel guilty about having things that others don't. I'm happy with very little, so why try for more?

   YES   NO

5. I focus on what could go wrong with a new business or love affair.

   YES   NO

6. I feel afraid to ask someone to help me achieve my goal.

   YES   NO

   Every "yes" answer indicates the presence of the settling-for-less sabotage strategy.

Settling for less can mean either that you don't believe you deserve to have more of life's abundance, or you feel guilty doing or having something that others don't. In any case, these negative thoughts create a focus on settling rather than on proactively going after the success you want.

8

▼

Giving Up Before You Start

The Resignation Sabotage Strategy

You gain strength, courage, confidence by every
experience in which you really stop to look fear
in the face . . . you must do the thing you think
you cannot.

—Eleanor Roosevelt

THE *RESIGNATION SABOTAGE strategy* is operating when you give up before you even begin a new love relationship, diet, career, or anything else that you want.

The kinds of statements I hear from people who are in resignation are: "There aren't any good men left, so why even look?" or "I'm not really good enough to get that new job, so why apply?" or "I know I'll never stick to that diet, so why should I starve myself?" All these statements are delivered with a huge, defeated sigh and a look of surrender. We're so effective at talking ourselves out of deserving more that we don't make any attempt to prove ourselves wrong.

The classic story of love at the supermarket speaks to this feeling. An attractive woman is standing in the checkout line at her neighborhood supermarket behind a tall, handsome guy. She sees him and starts thinking, "Oh, he'd be fun to go out with, he looks athletic, we could go walking together and bike riding. I wonder if he likes to dance." She's feeling positive and happy. Then the spoiler thoughts come in: "He'd probably leave me like my last boyfriend and never tell me why. Then I'd cry and be upset for another six months. Who needs it? He's not that cute anyway."

The man, who's now finished paying for his groceries, turns and sees the attractive woman behind him. He gives her a genuinely warm smile and says, "Hi, how are you doing today?" She scowls at him and snaps rudely, "Okay." The relationship is over before it can ever begin!

Why do we use this sabotage strategy? Why do we talk ourselves out of what we want? What fears do we cook up in our unconscious to spoil our dreams?

Our fears are as varied as our circumstances, but some of the pervasive ones in the resignation strategy are fear of failure, fear of success, fear of taking responsibility, fear of being overwhelmed, and fear of the amount of difficulty involved in attaining what we yearn for. Negative self-talk then eats away at our resolve by feeding those fears with "reasons" that they could be legitimate:

1. **Time**: "This (the career, the relationship, the diet) may take way too long to get going. I'm not sure I can do it."
2. **Difficulty**: "This might be so much harder than I think. I'm not sure all the effort will be worth it."
3. **Responsibility**: "I'm afraid I can't meet all the demands here and be accountable for getting this done."
4. **Overwhelming feelings**: "I won't be able to handle all this and still balance my life."

Linda's Internal Glass Ceiling

Linda had reached a level in her career where she kept hitting her head on her own internal glass ceiling. Her resignation sabotage had her feeling simply overwhelmed until she realized how she was sabotaging her career.

Linda is a very bright, energetic woman who wanted to be a success in her company. She was an excellent manager who always put her customers first and always gave attentive service. Every year she set high goals for her sales efforts, and every year she failed to reach them.

As I talked her through her self-sabotage script, she realized that as soon as she set a goal, she would tell herself: "But if I reach it, I really won't have any time for my family." That belief—for which there was no proof—made her subtly, unconsciously stop selling and start sabotaging her career advancement, giving up before she even tried.

When Linda was able to see that her negative beliefs about being successful *and* having a happy family life were the problem, she shifted her beliefs from "either/or" thinking to "both/and" thinking. This changed her feelings of being overwhelmed and raised her Deserve Level quickly and substantially. At a company party a few months later, she was awarded the number one sales position in her company—while her entire family proudly applauded from the audience.

The feeling that a goal is too difficult to achieve is a common one. Many of my clients resign themselves to mediocrity because it just seems too hard to take on a new goal, let alone a grand one. This is particularly true when it comes to goals related to weight and exercise.

I've been an expert on resignation around exercise. Every year in January I would decide that I needed to be in better shape, so I'd sign up at a gym. I eventually belonged to five gyms. I didn't go, I just gave them money. I was tithing to the gyms; they were my charity!

I gave up before I started because I'd tell myself "It seems too hard," or "It'll take too much time," or "I won't be in town to do it." Excuses, excuses, and more excuses. I wish I could tell you I've *completely* handled this self-sabotage around exercise. I'm doing much better, but I still have to work on it.

The Tyranny of the "What-Ifs?"

Angela worked in a clinic whose director wanted to raise its profile
and expand its reach in the community. He hoped this would also
enable him to expand the staff by drawing more prominent people
in the field to come work there. He'd worked with Angela for several
years and found her to be extremely capable and knowledgeable. He
wanted her to be chairperson of the clinic's accreditation committee—in fact, he thought she was the perfect choice for that position
and was willing to give her an initial boost in salary.

The job, which would take about two years, would entail coor-
dinating various reports from all the department heads in the clinic,
interviewing clinicians and patients regarding pluses and minuses
in the clinical program, and assessing and reporting on the quality
of the training in the educational program. Angela would then have
to collate all this material into a report that would go to the state
accreditation board as part of applying for state certification.

At first, Angela was excited and flattered. She agreed with the
director that her particular skills suited her well for the various tasks
involved in the project. She said she'd like to think about it overnight,
though; he appreciated her being so thoughtful about his offer.

That night Angela began picturing what would be required of
her—all the people and personalities she'd be dealing with, all the
fine-tuning of reports—and realized she could, indeed, do all of it.
Then she began to self-sabotage with her old "what-ifs." She'd never
done such a big or important project before now, and she thought,
"What if I can't really figure out how to do it?" "What if I miss
something important, and we have to do everything all over again?"
"What if I don't do it the way the other clinics have done it, and we
don't get accredited? Then it'll be my fault, and everyone will think
I've let them down!" "What if I do it all just fine, but we don't get
accredited anyway because someone doesn't want us to? Then I'll be
blamed for not finding a way around that!"

The next morning, Angela met with the director and turned
down the job because she just didn't want to be accountable—didn't
want the responsibility—if the clinic failed to get accredited. She

never really stopped to consider the excellent standing the clinic already had, the faith the director (and others) had in her ability, the amount of help that would be available to her because everyone wanted this to happen, or the great pleasure she'd have in being responsible for moving the clinic onto a new level! She gave up before she started, then watched the person who took the job succeed not only in getting the accreditation, but ultimately in becoming the assistant clinical director.

There are two Deserve Dilemmas that affect our ability to get started on what we want. These dilemmas have us resigning ourselves before we open our minds to the possibilities. They keep us stuck in resignation sabotage if we don't address them directly.

1. Our inability to ask for what we want
2. The kind and amount of guilt we have

I cannot reinforce for you enough that these Deserve Dilemmas are programmed by the beliefs and permissions we carry from our past. Our ability to *ask for what we want* is a primary issue in raising our Deserve Level.

Ask and Receive

Why is it so hard to ask? Many of my clients—especially professional women at all levels—have a terrible time asking for help, assistance, money, or support for what they want. We all somehow feel we have to do it ourselves. We should know everything and be able to use our own resources to meet all of our needs. Baloney! It's not possible in this complex world to meet all our own needs; like it or not, we are dependent beings.

Most of the fear of asking comes from our fear of rejection. We tell ourselves scary stories about what other people mean when they say no to us; the challenge is to reframe those stories into something more positive. Anytime I want to change my inner dialogue about the meaning of *no*, I think of Aunt Ethel.

Aunt Ethel invites you to join her for Thanksgiving dinner. You accept without hesitation because Aunt Ethel is your favorite aunt and the best cook in the whole world. Thanksgiving morning, you skip breakfast and lunch so you've got room for more of Aunt Ethel's homemade food.

When dinner comes around, Aunt Ethel is at the top of her game. The turkey is tender and moist, the mashed potatoes are fluffy and buttered to perfection, and the cornbread stuffing is out of this world. You gobble up everything in sight. Just as you're pushing your chair back from your second giant serving, Aunt Ethel tiptoes to your side and whispers, "Surprise! I saved the last slice of pumpkin pie just for you!"

You look up to see a beaming Aunt Ethel holding a thick slice of your favorite pumpkin pie. No one makes pumpkin pie like Aunt Ethel. You stare at the freshly baked pie, watching the scoop of vanilla ice cream melt from the heat.

But you're so full you can't eat another bite, so you smile politely and raise your hands in surrender. "Aunt Ethel, I love your pie, but I'm just too stuffed to eat a single bite. I can't believe I'm saying no, but right now I'm just too full."

"Oh, that's okay, dear," smiles Aunt Ethel. "I'll just wrap it up and you can take it with you."

The next day you open the refrigerator, and there's that slice of mouthwatering pumpkin pie just waiting for you. You're so hungry you can't stand it! You pour a big glass of milk and sit down to savor the pie that you've been thinking about for the last twenty-four hours. Much to your amazement, it's even better than you had imagined!

You call Aunt Ethel and thank her for the pie, and you're both happy as clams. She gave the gift of the pie, but when you said no, she didn't interpret it as a rejection. Instead, she understood that at the moment you were too full to accept her gift.

Likewise, people's lives are sometimes too full to accept the gift of joining you in a relationship or a business opportunity. Their lives may be too full of problems, kids, projects, or other demands. And when that's the case, all the energy and attention you'd want them to provide wouldn't be available anyway. So remember: when they refuse your gift, it's not the same as refusing *you*.

When people's lives are too full to accept your offers, their refusals are about them, not you. If they're hungry, the answer is yes; if they're full, the answer is no. Wrap up the pie and offer it again when they're hungry.

The Asking "Setup"

Mark Victor Hansen and Jack Canfield, in their excellent book *The Aladdin Factor*, talk about how we need to approach asking:

1. **Have a positive expectation.** *Ask as if you expect to get it. Assume that whatever you want, you can have. Don't assume before you ask that the answer is no.*
2. **Keep asking.** *If you don't get a yes the first time, keep asking. Being tenacious is one of the hallmarks of success.*
3. **Make your request clear and specific.** *The more vague you are, the easier it is to say no to you. "I'd like to have dinner with you on Friday night" is a lot more clear than "Let's get together sometime."*

Hansen and Canfield also suggest this daily exercise to restart our asking ability. Ask yourself:

- *"What did I want that I did not ask for today?"*
- *"Who could have helped me today if I'd asked?"*
- *"Where could I have asked for what I wanted and gotten it today?"*
- *"How could I have asked more effectively?"*

Once you receive an answer, create a new image of yourself actually asking for what you wanted. Visualize yourself asking for it more effectively. See yourself doing it the way you would have liked to had you not been so shy, frightened, prideful, or defensive. You'll be surprised how readily both the circumstances and the "corrections" will come to you.

What this activity does for you is heighten your awareness, which is the first step to all behavioral change. It also programs your unconscious to help you act more assertively and effectively in the future. Make this a daily ritual until you see your behavior changing.

For a wonderful example of positive expectancy and frequency in asking, we have Jeff and Stephanie. My good friend Stephanie's husband, Jeff, asked her ten times to marry him. Every time he asked her, they were in a different romantic spot—dinner on the French Riviera, sailing through the Sydney Bridge, at the Colosseum in Rome. She finally said yes and probably would have said it earlier, but she enjoyed the exciting process of being asked. They both enjoyed that excitement, along with his commitment to keep asking until he heard the word yes.

Chris Starts Asking

"I'm sixty! How in the world can I find a new career? No one will hire me at this age."

Chris was a talented upper-level manager in a large corporation. He loved his career and managed people with great care and skillfulness, but along with several other people in his company, he lost his job through a corporate merger. Chris came to see me because he couldn't find the energy to get started on a new career. He'd gone on interviews with a halfhearted spirit, feeling quite certain the company in question wouldn't want him. He resigned himself to early retirement as many of his colleagues were doing, but he wasn't happy. His depression spread to his family life, and his wife was increasingly unhappy with having him home all day.

Chris had sabotaged himself with *resignation*. As we talked about what had given him the greatest satisfaction in his previous jobs, he discovered that he loved daily interaction with people—feeling he was an integral part of building a team and inspiring people around him to work toward a common goal. After we had talked at some length and in some detail, he decided to reinvent himself.

He started telling everyone what he was looking for—an exciting, interactive work environment—and asking for help in finding it. Through a series of contacts, Chris found a small start-up company, is now happily engaged in helping build it, and is planning on working forever.

Guilt Aids and Abets Self-Sabotage

The second Deserve Dilemma that can keep us stuck in resignation sabotage is set up by the kind and amount of guilt we have. Let me first differentiate between the two different kinds: *appropriate guilt* and *inappropriate guilt.*

Appropriate guilt is the feeling of concern, worry, and embarrassment that accompanies our awareness that we've done something improper, like spilling coffee on a friend's new suit; or inadvertently hurting someone's feelings with a tired, cranky remark; or backing into another car and smashing its door; or stepping on someone's foot. We didn't mean to offend or hurt, but we can see the negative outcome that resulted and we feel bad. Healthy people take responsibility for their actions and make the appropriate amends.

Inappropriate guilt is another matter altogether. My colleague Hannah gave me a perfect example of this. Many years ago, at the end of a therapy session, she was walking a new client to the door. They were chatting, and because Hannah was carrying a stack of files, she didn't see the small office table until she had tripped over it, spilling the files onto the floor. Before she could even bend down, her client was on the floor nervously scooping them up and muttering, "Oh, I'm sorry, I'm so sorry, I'm so sorry."

Hannah kept trying to assure the client that she had absolutely nothing to do with dropping the files, that Hannah was the one who had tripped and dropped them. But, she told me, it was almost as if the client was in a trance and convinced that, if those files were on the floor, surely it was somehow *her* fault.

Hannah's client was awash in inappropriate guilt. This kind of guilt is the pervasive sense that we're to blame, that we're at fault for whatever problem is being presented to us. It's the *mea culpa* ("I am guilty") mentality.

We do not choose inappropriate guilt; it's inflicted upon us by others. The origins of inappropriate guilt usually lie with parents or other authority figures who used their power as a control device. (Hannah told me that her client's mother, for example, had virtually trained her client to believe that "no matter what you do, it's not enough"; in other words, "*you're* not enough.") After years of being blamed, judged, and even manipulated, we internalize the ability to do it to ourselves and to others.

Guilt, in general, starts with a feeling of self-blame (which is appropriate) or self-condemnation (which is inappropriate) after something has happened. The next feeling is either the need to make amends (which is appropriate and powerful) or to be shamed or punished (which is inappropriate and disempowering).

Inappropriate guilt, by its very nature, though, creates fear and anxiety and cannot coexist with loving feelings. Either we blame ourselves or—out of our own anxiety—we look around for someone else to blame. If we project blame onto others and deny any responsibility for our actions, that's a reflection of our own feelings of low self-esteem. Over time, the projection of these negative feelings pushes away our family, friends, children, and associates. Thus we become classic victims, our Deserve Level sinks to the bottom of some vast abyss, and we give up before we start. We become experts at resignation.

When you feel guilty, ask yourself, "Do I have the freedom to say no here?" Paradoxically, if the answer is yes, you're halfway out of feeling guilty. Here are some additional questions to ask yourself when you feel guilty:

1. What do I want?
2. To whom do I feel I can't say no without being punished?
3. To whom can I say no and still feel accepted?

Deserving More Money: The Fountain of Prosperity

A client I'll call Jane Allison tells this story:

> I used to have a recurring fantasy every time I went up to an ATM. I imagined it would say "Declined! You have no more money at all."
>
> Visions of myself as a bag lady on the streets of Los Angeles flooded my mind, even though these thoughts were completely

unfounded. I felt guilty about the prospect of having money and being the success I wanted to be. I was resigned to being mediocre. But in the past ten years I've gone from my bag-lady fear to being the co-owner of a lovely, successful business.

It wasn't an easy transition. I needed to give up a lot of mindless things I used to spend my time doing, to learn to focus, to move myself beyond my perceived wall of fear. I was resigned to the idea that I couldn't handle money. I needed to change my self-talk, needed to learn not to give up on myself before I tried to learn more.

When I first met my husband, Ted, I realized he had (and still has) the most healthy and inspiring attitude about money of anyone I'd ever met. He loves money, he thinks it's great. He doesn't believe that money is the root of all evil; instead it represents freedom, choices, and generosity.

He envisions himself as a "fountain of prosperity" with all the money he makes flowing up through him, sprinkling and splashing on all those close to him. When he told me this, I was delighted by his view and realized that I had a tremendous amount to learn from this man. I set about learning all I could, and in the past ten years I've been able to blast through my money fears. I've learned real estate, mortgages, investments, banking, corporations, and business in ways I never dreamed possible. His healthy attitude and the new permission he instilled in me created more self-confidence with money.

Once I accepted that money is a gift, once I allowed money to flow into my life, I saw it bring pleasure to others and myself in ways I'd never imagined.

Money, wealth, and value—these are often difficult areas in women's lives. Our attitudes about money are related to issues of deserving. Why don't we value ourselves more in this arena? In many households, women manage family bills and the checkbook, and yet we minimize our strengths in this area. Women are savers rather than investors, often out of fear there will not be enough money or resources to get by.

As the nurturers we are, we deserve freedom, luxury, safety, comfort, and security. We deserve to be free of guilt about having all those, right?

Right.

It's time for me to value myself as a woman who is skilled in the realm of money, to give myself confidence and acknowledge myself for my abilities.

It's time to let myself know that I am also good at this financial stuff, that I've learned a lot, and that I'm worthy of my own approval.

It's time to value my own financial knowledge and strength. I deserve to have money, enjoy money, and be successful with it.

If you think you might have a resignation sabotage strategy, that you're someone who gives up before you start, complete this exercise:

▶ **Exercise: The Resignation Sabotage Strategy**

I give up on my goals because:

_____

_____

_____

I tell myself (check the ones that apply to you):

_____ My goals are too hard.

_____ My goals are too time-consuming.

_____ I won't be successful anyway.

_____ If I'm successful, it will mess up my life.

_____ I don't deserve success.

_____ I'll be overwhelmed by success.

_____ I'll feel guilty if I'm successful.

The more sentences you checked, the more likely you are to be using the resignation sabotage strategy.

9

▼

I Messed Up

The Fatal-Flaw Sabotage Strategy

WHAT WAS I THINKING?

—Bill Clinton

THE *FATAL-FLAW* FORM of self-sabotage is a psychological trait or personality problem that undoes all our best efforts. On the surface everything seems fine, but underneath the veneer a *fatal flaw* is eating away at the groundwork of our lives. The fatal flaw can be perfectionism, procrastination, narcissism, untreated depression, rage, or any other untreated personality problem that spoils a person's life. A stressful event occurs, the pressure builds, and the fatal-flaw sabotage erupts into the light of day. This particular sabotage strategy can bring down the entire structure of our lives and needs dedicated effort to change.

Perfectionism

"Do it right or don't do it at all!"

"If I can't be number one, there's no point in trying. Everyone knows what number two is."

"If I don't do things perfectly, I'm a loser."

"It's just not acceptable to make a mistake."

All of these messages combine to form the chorus of perfectionism. Perfectionists ignore the 95 percent that's right about their lives and focus on the 5 percent that's "wrong" (particularly about themselves). We disregard the beautiful dress and shoes we're wearing to the party and obsess about that tiny blemish on our cheek.

As I write this, I can hear that annoying, self-critical voice in my head: "Are you sure you said that correctly? You'd better not write about perfectionism in an improper way!"

As with all self-sabotaging behaviors, perfectionism occurs in varying degrees. You can be a "perfectionist-lite" and be a little annoyed at your behavior and performance, or you can be the "perfectionist on steroids," constant criticism and judgments about your inadequacies running a perpetual relay race in your head.

You might be asking, "Well, shouldn't we try to do things perfectly or at least give our best effort?" The answer is yes, we *should* strive for excellence—but not perfection. You need to give yourself a certain amount of leeway for human mess-ups and mistakes. Accept the inevitable: we're all descended from a long line of human beings, and none of them was perfect. Alcoholics Anonymous compassionately reminds its members that "progress, not perfection" is the measure for assessing oneself.

If you're someone who uses perfectionism as a stick rather than a carrot, you'll notice certain characteristics about yourself: constant worrying about mistakes; inflexibility; feelings of pressure to perform well from yourself or others; and an inability to celebrate the successes you do have.

I'm reminded of that anecdote about how parental messages fuel perfectionism. A man excitedly calls his father with the news: "Dad, Dad, I just won the Nobel Prize for curing cancer!" His father pauses and replies, "What about heart disease?"

That's the heart of the perfectionist's dilemma—it's never good enough; in other words, "*I'm* not good enough." Or "No matter what I do, it's (*I'm*) not enough."

Here are some characteristics of the perfectionist:

- You have a fear of change and hesitate to take a risk because it might not be "good enough," or worse, it might not be the absolute best choice.
- You're very self-absorbed, always worried about what people are thinking about you, so you're constantly judging and evaluating your performance as if through someone else's eyes.
- You're not having much fun, spontaneity, or joy.
- You have an abiding fear of failure and fear of rejection ("If I'm not perfect, I'll be a failure and people will reject me.")
- Along with being your own harshest critic, you're constantly judging the imperfections and failings of others.
- You believe there's some state of perfection you could reach "if only I wouldn't mess up or make mistakes."
- You have a reason to fear success: "If I reach my goal, will I be able to maintain that level of achievement?"

If you grade yourself by a perfectionist standard, every day is finals week. You're chronically anticipating a report card, and you're not an *A* student. Most achievement-oriented people have some of these tendencies, but the issue is one of degree.

Body Perfectionism

Debbie said she had always been big. Well, tall anyway, and certainly not thin. She'd always felt a bit larger than life. From fourth grade on, she was the tallest, heaviest, and biggest kid in her school. By eighth grade she was her full adult height, five feet nine inches tall. Every year the school nurse went from classroom to classroom, measuring and weighing each kid while the other kids waited in line and watched. And every year, when it was Debbie's turn, a gasp went out through the line as her statistics were made public; the information always rippled quickly through the entire school. She wasn't actually fat, but she was mature for her age, the size of a full-grown adult woman.

From the time Debbie was a little girl, she loved dance and music. Because she felt such great joy moving her body and singing, it seemed that must be her path in life. She read books about dancers throughout history and imagined she was Isadora Duncan. She took lessons in ballet, jazz, and tap. But while her dancer's heart was being filled with inspiration and dreams, her dancer's body was growing taller and taller.

Taller than all the boys and male dancers, Debbie loomed especially large because she was surrounded by diminutive female dancers. Yet she loved the whole endeavor so much she tried to override the—to her—obvious fact that she just didn't have a dancer's body.

She even enrolled in college as a dance major, hoping to find a niche for a large choreographer or tall soloist. But there she was, attending the University of Hawaii, where 90 percent of the women in the dance department were of Asian descent and quite dainty, averaging five feet tall and weighing ninety pounds. And here, too, she towered over the men. She felt out of place, not good enough to deserve a role on stage as a featured dancer. Because of her perfectionistic standards she wouldn't let herself try out for the roles she really wanted.

Now, as she looks back at pictures of herself at that age, she sees she was tall and solid, but not at all fat—or even really very big. Yet she'd thought she was rather ugly and extremely fat at most stages of her life. Her ideal of what a perfect dancer should be held her back from really going after her dream.

In myself and in most women I've met, the issue of size has to do with power and presence—and is the source of some horrible wounding. Whatever the origin of that wounding, whether it's the media portraying us as skinny things or fashion magazines displaying images of femaleness that are impossible to achieve, at some point in their lives most women have terribly poor and terribly distorted physical self-esteem. We believe that some elusive external perfection is the ultimate standard for being accepted and appreciated. I know I'm not alone in this; I've yet to meet a woman who is completely happy with her body.

As we grow older and wiser, many of us are working to embrace the idea that we're "perfect" just the way we are. Still, it can be a long, hard climb out of this particularly deep hole into which we sink when we don't believe we deserve to claim what we want.

As for Debbie, she has matured, let go of those perfectionistic standards, and finally accepted how lovely she is. All her dance training has also enabled her to move through the world with a grace and elegance most of us will never achieve.

Procrastination: The Scarlett O'Hara Syndrome

In the classic film *Gone with the Wind*, the character of Scarlett O'Hara is famous for the way she postpones dealing with things that are important. "I'll think about that tomorrow" is her chief coping mechanism.

All our lives we've heard that "procrastination is the thief of time," and that continues to be true. While appearing to be working hard, we can literally be giving our life and income away in small chunks. Procrastination is a fatal flaw and an ultra-sneaky sabotage strategy.

Have you ever had the experience of doing *anything* instead of the task at hand? Many, many people have told me they procrastinate even on the most important tasks. They do the tasks they prefer, then feel angry, frustrated, and resentful because they didn't get the "real" tasks done.

While I began to write this book, I was a master of procrastination. I set aside every Friday morning to write. I'd get up and go to work at about 8:30 A.M. I'd sit at my desk and notice I didn't have any pencils sharpened, so I'd go do that (even in this age of computers, you can't write without sharpened pencils, you know). Then I'd get my notes in order, but the phone would ring, and I'd answer it! Then, after I'd taken care of whatever it was, I was ready to go back to writing, but I needed to warm up my coffee. On my way back from the kitchen I'd notice that all the shoes were out of order in my closet and think, "It'll just take a minute to get them in order . . . " The phone would ring again. I'd answer and talk for fifteen minutes, then I'd be a little hungry so I'd go to the kitchen for a snack. Got the picture? It would be 10:00 A.M.—I'd been "at work" on my book for one and a half hours without having written a word!

I subscribe to psychologist David Premack's theory that procrastination occurs when people gorge themselves on activities they prefer to the tasks they need to do. They become so involved in these more preferred activities that they eventually have no time or energy left for less preferred tasks or projects (usually the most important ones). Although these people have been very busy, they haven't been productive.

To resolve this situation, Premack suggests using preferred activities as rewards. In simple terms, you must do some work on the less preferred tasks before engaging in the more preferred activities. For example, you must work on your book for at least thirty minutes before going to your favorite Internet site as a reward. If you decide to go online first, you'll continue to delay the work on your book.

Premack suggests breaking big tasks into small increments of twenty to thirty minutes, then giving yourself a five- to ten-minute reward. Using this technique conscientiously, you can work on tasks all day long, then celebrate your accomplishments at the end of the day.

Narcissism: How Great I Am!

The character of Narcissus in Greek legend was so completely captivated by his own reflection in a pool of water that he fell in and drowned. That story gives us the name of this form of fatal-flaw sabotage. People with a narcissistic personality disorder act from a sense of self-loathing and a dread of failure, coupled with the inability to endure shame, the emotional fallout of failure. But you would never know it by looking at them.

Roughly one million people are affected by narcissistic personality disorder, and millions more suffer from narcissistic tendencies. Among the traits they may have are:

- An inflated feeling of self-importance
- An absence of genuine self-esteem (because a big chunk of their identity is missing)
- A kind of seductive charisma that seems to engage others but doesn't truly relate to them
- A deep, abiding fear of being controlled

- A magnetic charm that brings people to them until such people no longer serve a purpose
- A feeling of exemption from many "rules" the rest of us agree to follow
- A desperate need for admiration—with a simultaneous defense against being really "seen" by anyone
- An insensitivity to the feelings, thoughts, and needs of others

"What Was I Thinking?"

In his autobiography, *My Life*, Bill Clinton writes about the costs of leading walled-off, parallel lives: "If you had the kind of childhood I did, and you had to get up every day and put your game face on, you'd become a secret-keeper like I did."

He said he deeply regretted his affair with Monica Lewinsky:

> *I was misleading everyone about my personal feelings. I was embarrassed and wanted to keep it from my wife and daughter, and I didn't want the American people to know I'd let them down. . . .*
>
> *What was I thinking? No matter how mad or scared I was about what else was going on, why in the world did I do that? And how can I make it up to everybody involved, beginning with Hillary and Chelsea, my administration, and the American people? That was by far the most difficult thing. What I had to work on in my own mind was not letting my sense of being on the right side of the fight get in the way of my need to examine why in the living daylights I'd done that [with Lewinsky]—and what I should do to work through it.*

Clinton's fatal flaws of narcissism and perfectionism fused together to generate his unique and costly self-sabotage. The narcissistic need to present an image of being perfect contributed to Clinton's hiding his flaws and being a secret-keeper. This need to hide his flaws created a split between his real self and his hidden life. That hidden life developed its own set of rules—and while in it, Clinton lost perspective and began to feel exempt from the natural and logical consequences that certain behaviors would bring upon the rest of us.

Martha Stewart: From Big Fish to Big House

In another amazing public example of a fatal-flaw sabotage, Martha Stewart was judged guilty on all four charges in the ImClone stock-trading case against her.

Stewart was convicted on one count of conspiracy, two counts of making false statements, and one count of obstruction of agency proceedings. The charges were built on allegations that she sold ImClone stock after she got an inside tip from her broker, then lied about it to protect herself and her company.

But why did Martha lie? The money she made by selling her ImClone stock was chump change for a billionaire. What she lost in becoming a felon, doing time in prison, and tarnishing her image was worth far more.

She lied because she thought she could get away with it. The fatal flaw of narcissism (overwhelming pride, arrogance, the sense of being exempt) creates havoc in many famous people's lives. The cult of celebrity and its adjunct feelings of entitlement inflate many egos: "I'm [fill in famous name]. I don't have to play by the same rules as everyone else."

This feeling of being entitled to redefine a set of legal or moral rules to suit your actions is a by-product of narcissistic pride. Narcissism was Martha's fatal flaw, and it landed her in jail.

Untreated Depression: A Powerful Fatal Flaw

Untreated depression is another fatal flaw that has created many a meltdown. Although the term *depression* is commonly used to describe a temporary depressed mood—when one is sad or down or "feels blue"—clinical depression is a serious illness involving the body, mind, and thoughts in a way that can't simply be willed or wished away. It's often a disabling disease that affects a person's work, school, family and social relationships, sleeping and eating habits, general health, and ability to enjoy life.

The course of clinical depression varies widely: it can be a once-in-a-lifetime event or have multiple recurrences; it can appear either gradually or suddenly; and it can last for a few months or become a lifelong disorder.

Clinical depression is a common psychiatric disorder that can manifest in a variety of symptoms, and someone suffering from it won't necessarily have all those symptoms. However, almost all sufferers display a marked change in mood, a deep feeling of sadness, and a noticeable "flatlining"—a loss of interest or pleasure in favorite activities. Other symptoms include (as stated in Mayoclinic.com):

- Persistent sad, anxious, or "empty" mood
- Loss of appetite and/or weight loss—or conversely, overeating and weight gain
- Insomnia, early-morning awakening, or oversleeping
- Restlessness or irritability
- Feelings of worthlessness, inappropriate guilt, or helplessness
- Feelings of hopelessness and pessimism
- Difficulty thinking, concentrating, remembering, or making decisions
- Thoughts of death or suicide, or suicide attempts
- Loss of interest or pleasure in hobbies and activities that were once enjoyed, including sex
- Decreased energy, fatigue, feeling "slowed down" or sluggish
- Persistent physical symptoms that do not respond to treatment, such as headaches, digestive disorders, and chronic pain

The severity of symptoms varies widely from person to person. However, with the exception of suicidal thoughts or attempts, symptoms must persist for at least two weeks before they can be considered a potential sign of depression.

According to the National Institute of Mental Health:

- Depressive disorder is the leading cause of disability in the United States for people between the ages of fifteen and forty-four.
- Depressive disorder affects approximately 14.8 million American adults, or about 6.7 percent of the U.S. population aged eighteen and older in a given year.

- Depressive disorder can develop at any age, but the median age at onset is thirty-two.
- Depressive disorder is more prevalent in women than in men.

Mike Wallace

Mike Wallace of "60 Minutes" has informed, startled, and incensed millions with his documentaries—but he hasn't always handled the corresponding criticism effectively.

In 1982 his documentary on our government's misrepresentation of the number of enemy troops during the Vietnam War inspired an American general to file a libel suit. In reaction, Wallace developed psychosomatic pain: a feeling of "knives" in his arms and weakness in his legs. Soon he was battling suicidal thoughts and relying on sleeping pills for rest.

When the trial finally began in 1984, Wallace collapsed and was hospitalized for two weeks. His doctor diagnosed him with clinical depression and gave him the drug Ludiomil; the stress of the trial had revealed an underlying chemical imbalance that had led to depression. When the trial finally ended in 1985, Wallace was able to stop taking medication, but he suffered two more bouts of depression over the next ten years.

Wallace appeared in the 1998 HBO documentary *Dead Blue: A Film About Surviving Depression*. The film begins with him describing the illness as "a dark cloud that descended upon me." He refers to his depression as a by-product of his professional life and of having his credibility challenged in front of the media and the world. It affected his self-esteem and self-concept and made him criticize his entire sense of himself. He felt utterly defeated during his depressive episodes and speaks of this time as a very emotional period in his life.

His wife recounts her desperation and frustration in trying to help him during his depressive episodes. She felt that he became a stranger during those times, that she lost him and went through her own kind of grief process. Wallace concludes that the combination of being in psychotherapy and regularly taking medication since 1993 has helped him keep his depression under control.

Mike Wallace's depression might have turned into a fatal flaw if he hadn't taken such courageous steps to handle it—indeed, he could have sabotaged his entire career. Instead he stepped up, got help, and has become an advocate for destigmatizing the illness.

▶ **Exercise: Fatal Flaw Rating**

Rate yourself on the scale in the following areas, and write in others that might concern you.

Perfectionist Rating

Lowest   1   2   3   4   5   6   7   8   9   10   Highest

Procrastination Rating

Lowest   1   2   3   4   5   6   7   8   9   10   Highest

Narcissistic Rating

Lowest   1   2   3   4   5   6   7   8   9   10   Highest

Depression Rating

Lowest   1   2   3   4   5   6   7   8   9   10   Highest

Any other "fatal flaws" that concern you:

_____

Lowest   1   2   3   4   5   6   7   8   9   10   Highest

Other personality problems such as addictions (alcoholism, addiction to drugs, being a workaholic or a "shopaholic," eating disorders, and so on) or unmanaged anger can also function as fatal flaws when they go unrecognized and untreated.

Fatal flaws are the sabotages, the profound deal-killers, that ultimately trip us up as we're racing to the finish line. They can be surprisingly subtle and unconscious, but they are the roadblocks that keep us spinning back into negative behaviors.

As with all sabotage strategies, the intensity of these behaviors is important. Whatever area you rated the highest is the one where you most need to improve your Deserve Level.

10

▼

Denial Divas

The Denial Sabotage Strategy

THE WORST LIES ARE THE LIES WE TELL OURSELVES. WE
LIVE IN DENIAL OF WHAT WE DO, EVEN WHAT WE THINK.
WE DO THIS BECAUSE WE'RE AFRAID.
> —Richard Bach

DECADES AFTER JUDY Garland and Marilyn Monroe descended into
the abyss of drugs and alcohol—and finally suicide—their fans are
still haunted by the dual tragedies of those lives cut short. Recently,
in the pictures of Britney Spears emerging from one of her frequent self-sabotage events, we see a defeated woman. We also see an
unglamorous Lindsay Lohan being booked on a DUI. These "denial
divas" will sabotage their careers and lives if they don't permanently
stop denying their problems and get help.

Ever since the day David beat Goliath, humans have been fas-
cinated by people who fell short when they had everything in place
to win. If you're human, you're capable of being a denial diva about
something—your stress, your job, your relationship, your weight,
your health. It's in our nature to want everything to be fine, so denial
functions as a gloss over the harsh realities of life.

Denial is defined in psychological terms as a defense mechanism that processes anxiety by keeping us disconnected from the outer and inner reality of our lives. In other words, we ignore or refuse to believe what's going on around and within us.

In terms of immediate survival, denial serves momentarily to protect our psychological well-being in traumatic situations—or in any circumstance that threatens to overwhelm us. But as a sabotage strategy, it operates very much to our detriment. The more you fear you don't deserve something you want, the more denial you have to use. For example: "I'm afraid I won't get that promotion, so a couple of drinks will make me feel better." "My husband yelled at me again, and I was afraid this marriage just isn't going to work, so I went out and bought a thousand-dollar purse."

The unconscious fear that you can't be, do, or have what you want is the push to acting out this sabotage strategy. The breakthrough comes when you admit the fears and stop running from them.

There are many examples of denial in our lives:

- **Minimizing:** Minimizing is admitting the problem to some degree but in such a way that you've made it seem much less serious or significant than it actually is. "Yes, I drink, but not that much," or "I'm having a few problems at work," are frequently heard examples of minimizing.
- **Rationalizing:** Rationalizing is making excuses or giving reasons to justify your behavior. "I had a hard day and I was upset," or "You'd spend money too if you had a husband like mine," are some examples of rationalizing. You don't completely deny the behavior, but you give an inaccurate or incomplete explanation of its cause.
- **Intellectualizing or generalizing:** Intellectualizing is avoiding emotional, personal awareness of a problem by classifying it in a general or vague way. "People in other countries have wine with lunch, are they all alcoholics?" "My family is full of alcoholics, so I must have those genes." "My relationship with my father was so bad, no wonder I can't work for a male boss." These all are examples of intellectualizing.
- **Blaming:** Blaming (also called projecting) is maintaining that the responsibility for the behavior lies somewhere else, not with you.

"If you had my boss, you'd be angry too," and "I lost my job, so I went on a bender," are examples of blaming. You don't deny the behavior, but you place its cause "out there," not within yourself.

- **Diversion:** Diversion is changing the subject to avoid dealing with a topic that feels threatening to you: "My drinking bothers you? Well, your weight bothers me!" A common example of diversion is to respond with an attempt at humor, such as "Okay, you don't think I make enough money, so what's for dinner?"
- **Bargaining:** Bargaining involves cutting deals or setting conditions for when you'll be better able to deal with the problem, though those conditions never quite seem to materialize. For example: "I'll quit drinking if you quit smoking," or "I'll quit smoking when there's less stress at work."
- **Passivity:** Passivity is ignoring the situation or declaring yourself its victim: "There's nothing I can do," or "I've tried to quit smoking before, but it's stronger than me," or "If only I had more willpower . . ."

Daniel's Career Denial

Daniel is a confident, self-made man. He prided himself on the hard work that had made him successful. Throughout his career, his strength was in his perfectionist's attention to details. His ability to remember facts and figures made him the "go-to" person; he enjoyed solving workers' problems and making quick decisions. Coupled with his compulsive need for recognition, his skills had enabled him to rise through the corporate ranks. He was always on top of the work and always delivered results for his division.

But beneath this veneer, you could tell he didn't trust others to do things as well as he did. Daniel insisted on making all the decisions in order to ensure the organizations he managed were in control.

But losing control, the very thing he feared most, finally got him fired. Workers labeled him a micromanager who ultimately slowed them all down and kept them from doing their jobs efficiently. Eventually, after doing everything they could to coach Daniel into more productive thinking and cooperative behavior, top management concluded the business was out of control on the shop floor of his 350-employee division. Daniel's denial, narcissism, and perfectionism had created a blind spot and finally tripped him up. He had a kind of strength that turned against him because he couldn't see its downside.

Shocked and disillusioned, Daniel lamented to his wife, "They're so out of line, they just don't appreciate what I'm able to do!" She listened patiently to his rationalizations and finally said, "Daniel, for the past ten years I've been trying to talk to you about this very thing, but you've continually ignored me! You micromanage me, and you don't hear the kids when they tell you you're doing it to them, too. Now maybe you understand."

Toni's Tap Dancing

Denial is a form of dodging what we don't want to deal with. So, the question is: what are you pretending not to know?

My client Toni told me her story about denial. She worked in a major corporation, and for many years she had been the target of abusive comments from her boss. She had denied the effect on her work and mental health until one day she had a breakdown.

She said, "I'd go to work, and I'd put on cement shoes. I was unhappy and despondent, and everything I did had a heaviness to it. I finally realized my cement shoes were my unspoken thoughts and feelings. After I realized that, I wrote a letter to human resources telling them about my issue. They immediately responded and got me a new position. Now I'm working in a wonderful job climate. My cement shoes were my denial, and it took a lot to chip away at them. Why had I denied the abuse for so long?"

Because it is so automatic and unconscious, denial is also a primary psychological symptom of addiction. Addicts are often the last to recognize their disease, thus perpetuating the cycle even longer. Sadly, many addicts act out their addictions even while their world collapses around them—then blame everyone and everything but themselves for their problems.

We're all addicted! Our quick-fix culture is creating layers and layers of addicts. The thought goes like this: if you feel lonely, just have a dish of ice cream; if you're mad at your spouse, just go shopping; if you feel inadequate, then a couple of martinis will take that problem away in just a few minutes. The next morning, get yourself ready for the day with a triple-shot, nonfat latte. All of these behaviors are ways to deny our feelings and treat our pain with diversions and avoidance.

Many studies have supported the link between denial and addiction. Results of the National Household Survey on Drug Abuse, conducted by the Office of National Drug Control Policy, reveal that, while millions of Americans habitually smoke pot, drink alcohol, snort cocaine, and swallow prescription drugs, many drug users who meet the criteria for needing treatment don't even recognize they have a problem. The figure on those "in denial" is estimated at more than 4.6 million—a significantly higher number of individuals in need of professional help than had previously been thought.

What Is Addiction?

Addiction is defined by Aviel Goodman, M.D., as a process in which a behavior that can function both to produce pleasure and to provide escape from internal discomfort is employed in a pattern characterized by: (1) recurrent failure to control the behavior (powerlessness) and (2) continuation of the behavior despite significant negative consequences (unmanageability). Any recovering addict will tell you that it is the nature of every addiction to be "cunning, baffling, and powerful."

There are *substance* addictions and *process* addictions; both cause a person to become emotionally and psychologically hooked—and in the case of substance addictions, physically dependent as well. If you're addicted to a drug, whether it's legal or illegal, you experience intense cravings for it regardless of the obvious irrationality of continued use. An addict always wants "a little bit more." When you stop taking the drug, you're likely to have, among other things, unpleasant physical reactions.

An estimated 19.5 million Americans over the age of twelve use illicit drugs. Many other people abuse or are addicted to legal drugs like cigarettes and alcohol. While not everyone who uses drugs becomes addicted, many people do. As many as 19,000 people die of drug-related causes every year.

Drug addiction obviously involves compulsively using a substance, regardless of the potentially negative social, psychological, and physical consequences. But there are other forms of addiction, all of which involve denial—such as spending, gambling, shopping, and various eating disorders.

In Denial About Spending

Ashley is a stockbroker in New York City. Her days are intensely demanding and stressful. For years she had a pattern; when she got off work, she shopped. "I'd tell myself I work really hard, why shouldn't I buy Gucci jeans?" She did buy Gucci jeans, and Versace bags, and Prada shoes. If she'd owned a car, there'd have been a not-funny bumper sticker on it: "When the Going Gets Tough, the Tough Go Shopping."

Ashley was in debt up to her ears. She was living way beyond her income and denying that reality. When she felt stressed or powerless or low, she got high by spending money. She self-soothed and self-medicated by shopping.

When the monthly credit card bills arrived, she would retrieve them before her husband could see them. Whenever she reached the maximum on one card, she'd take immediate advantage of those dozens of offers that come in the mail and sign up for another one. The credit card companies were more than happy to collude with her.

This dance of denial continued until there was a family crisis that almost cost Ashley her marriage, and her debt could be a secret no longer. Once she had to face her denial sabotage, she also had to look at the many ways she used shopping and spending to mask a complex web of feelings—in her case, a mix of powerlessness, anxiety, and shame that had made it impossible for her *ever* to admit to herself or anyone else that she couldn't afford something.

Ashley embarked on a program that involved getting psychological insight into her addiction as well as taking very specific steps toward financial sobriety. She now lives a debt-free life with her husband and family.

Winona Acts Out

Why does a two-time Academy Award nominee steal more than $5,500 worth of high-fashion merchandise from the Beverly Hills Saks Fifth Avenue store when she could have easily paid cash for everything? During a weeklong trial, and after a little more than a day of jury deliberations, Winona Ryder was found guilty of grand theft. The actress thus became the star of her own self-inflicted denial drama.

For three years she had been filling thirty-seven prescriptions from twenty doctors under a half-dozen aliases. Her probation report concluded the actress was apparently addicted to painkillers.

Ryder wasn't convicted of any drug charges, and defense attorney Mark Geragos emphasized that she had prescriptions for eight medications on her when she was arrested. Geragos, who tried to keep the report sealed, told the judge Ryder had a "pain-management" problem. But the probation report suggested a different scenario.

Under the alias of "Emily Thompson," Ryder had been the patient of a doctor who wrote prescriptions for her under both names. All the personal information in the Thompson file was Ryder's, including a photocopy of her driver's license and an original patient form signed "Winona Ryder."

The authors of the probation report quoted police detective George Elwell as concluding Ryder had a drug problem and needed intervention: "He claimed, 'We don't want to find her slumped over in a car with a needle in her arm.'"

Superior Court Judge Elden Fox ordered the star of *Girl, Interrupted* and *Reality Bites* to pay $10,000 in fines and restitution and perform 480 hours of community service. She was also ordered to participate in a court-approved drug and psychological program.

"It is not my intention to make an example of you," Fox told Ryder. But he said she had disappointed many people and that she would have to "confront certain issues" that led to her behavior. "You have refused to accept personal responsibility," he told the actress.

By its very nature, denial doesn't even have personal responsibility on the radar screen.

Drug addiction removes people from—helps them deny—the reality of the present. Legal and illegal drugs can induce a range of feelings from euphoric to numb to suicidal. What starts out legiti-mately killing the pain of a hideous toothache can, in many people, turn into the only way to get through the days, weeks, and months long after the toothache is gone.

Until recently, even certain sectors of the medical and psychologi-cal field were in denial about the magnitude of the addiction problem in this country. Elizabeth, a colleague of mine, tells the story of being at a professional conference in the early 1990s. Over lunch at a group table, someone asked her what kind of practice she had. She said she worked with a wide variety of people, but recently had experienced more and more alcoholics and addicts coming in for treatment. To her shock, the man next to her—a fellow psychologist—asked haughtily, "Ugh, how can you stand to work with those people?!"

Elizabeth smiled and didn't miss a beat as she responded, "Well, you'd better be glad *somebody's* working with them, because 'those people' are managing *your* money at your investment firm."

Not only is each individual addict in denial and ultimately sabo-taging his or her career, but gathered together in sufficient numbers addicts can sabotage their company's future and threaten the stability of the larger economy. Again, I'm not talking just about drug addic-tion, but about process addictions as well. Does the name Enron mean anything to you?

Overweight Nation

Certainly, America is becoming an overweight nation. Our addiction to fast food, instant gratification, and sundry unhealthy lifestyles has kept us in denial of the long-term consequences of putting on much, much more than "a few extra pounds."

Here are the statistics: there are approximately 127 million obese and nine million severely obese people among us. Obesity is a complex disease involving environmental, genetic, metabolic, and psychological components. It's currently the second leading cause of preventable death in the United States.

The numbers continue to increase every year. Currently 64.5 percent of U.S. adults aged twenty and older are overweight, and 30.5 percent are obese. Obesity increases the risk of becoming ill from nearly thirty different serious medical conditions and is associated with an increase in deaths from all causes. At a minimum, half of the people in all age groups are overweight and at least 20 percent are obese.

Kirstie Alley gained national attention as Jenny Craig's former spokesperson with her seventy-plus pounds of weight loss. The star of "Fat Actress" lost her job because of losing her weight!

When asked how she put on all that weight, she answered that she was in denial about the extent of her weight gain. It was seeing a photo of herself that shocked her out of denial and into action. She's on the road to physical health and ending her self-sabotage.

▶ **Exercise: Addiction Denial**

If you are concerned that you might be in denial about an addiction to a substance, a process, and/or a behavior, ask yourself these questions:

1. Is this substance, process, and/or behavior an important part of your life?

   YES   NO

2. Do you spend much of the day thinking about it or doing it?

   YES   NO

3. Do you indulge in it in order to change the way you are feeling?

   YES   NO

4. Have you ever done it in secret?

   YES   NO

5. Does the thought of giving it up worry you?

   YES   NO

6. Do you react badly and become defensive when people suggest it's a problem?

   YES   NO

If the answer to any of these is yes, it could be time to start thinking about the changes you need to make to reduce—or altogether eliminate—your dependency. The first step is to get out of your denial and admit to yourself that you need help.

Next, reach out to a support group to help you through this—like Gamblers Anonymous, Alcoholics Anonymous, Narcotics Anonymous, Overeaters Anonymous, Debtors Anonymous, or any number of programs now available in communities all across the country. All twelve-step programs have available meetings composed of people with specific interests in common: certain professionals, executives, doctors, lawyers, nonsmokers, women only, men only, and so on.

You can also find other recovery support groups, as well as therapists and life coaches, who can help you look at how your career might be contributing to your addiction problems. Once you're out of denial and in recovery, it will be important to learn what to say and how to act in situations like going to a bar after work with your coworkers or your boss wanting you to go shopping with her during lunch.

Ever-increasing numbers of celebrities publicly admitting to an addiction have made the process a more forgiving one. Even though the paparazzi tend to sensationalize this problem and strip away the tremendous human pathos involved, we are nonetheless seeing the consequences of addiction writ large. We're reminded that fame and great wealth may mask internal demons for a while, but can't eliminate them; only by emerging from the darkness of denial into the full light of consciousness and clarity can the self-sabotage stop and a whole new life begin.

▼

PART III

I Deserve More!

11

▼

How You Run Your Life Is How You Run Your Business

OUR DEEPEST FEAR IS NOT THAT WE ARE INADEQUATE.
OUR DEEPEST FEAR IS THAT WE ARE POWERFUL BEYOND
MEASURE. IT IS OUR LIGHT, NOT OUR DARKNESS, THAT
MOST FRIGHTENS US. WE ASK OURSELVES, WHO AM I TO
BE BRILLIANT, GORGEOUS, TALENTED, AND FABULOUS?
ACTUALLY, WHO ARE YOU NOT TO BE? YOU ARE A CHILD
OF GOD. YOUR PLAYING SMALL DOESN'T SERVE THE
WORLD.

—Marianne Williamson

THE TITLE OF this chapter reflects a central idea: that you are at the center of your own universe. You aren't defined (unless you let yourself be) by your career, financial status, friends, or family. It's *you* running your life and your business.

At the heart of stopping self-sabotage lies the indispensable need to change our core belief that we aren't enough, that we don't deserve to get what we want. Carried with us from our past into our present, that belief violates the soul and sets up most of our self-sabotages. It also substantially lowers our Deserve Level.

As Eckhart Tolle so eloquently says in *A New Earth: Awakening to Your Life's Purpose:*

Why does the ego play roles? Because of one unexamined assumption, one fundamental error, one unconscious thought. That thought is: I am not enough. Other unconscious thoughts follow: I need to play a role in order to get what I need to be fully myself; I need to get more so that I can be more. But you cannot be more than you are because underneath your physical and psychological form, you are one with Life itself, one with Being. In form, you are and will always be inferior to some, superior to others. In essence, you are neither inferior nor superior to anyone. True self-esteem and true humility arise out of that realization. In the eyes of the ego, self-esteem and humility are contradictory. In truth, they are one and the same.

Deserving is a way of taking responsibility for your own power in a respectful, authentic way. *Power* is not to be confused with being controlling—the use of inauthentic power to dominate others—nor is *respectful* to be conflated with denying your own worth by underserving yourself. By saying "I deserve," you're asserting your right to want and to be "good enough" to achieve what you want.

You raise your Deserve Level by focusing your personal power on what you want. I've spent a lifetime learning how to do that. As a child I grew up witnessing a severe power imbalance at home. My father had all of it, and my mother was reduced to going along regardless of what she wanted.

This concept of power was to haunt me for years. I struggled with learning how to lay claim to a sense of my own power in ways that were neither dominating nor submissive—in other words, neither controlling nor passive-aggressive. I wanted my feelings to be heard and taken into account, and when they weren't, I felt ignored and run over. Then, rather than asserting what I truly wanted or believed, I'd react by being rebellious and refusing to go along with someone else's program. I knew I needed to learn to have power *with* others.

So, how have I consistently and respectfully shown myself and others that I deserve more? I take charge where I do have power: with myself and my interpretations of life events. I don't control other people or what happens, but I do control my *response* to both. I create a higher Deserve Level by embracing my own thoughts and feelings and rewriting my script.

This is not only a "how to," it's also a "why to." You're not raising your Deserve Level for the sake of your ego, you're raising it for the sake of your soul. All of us struggle with some wound that separates us from all that we can be, do, or have. Yet, paradoxically, this wound from our past generates in us the deep feeling that there's indeed more to us than we've managed to create thus far. This is the feeling that we deserve not simply more material things, but a deeper connection to ourselves and to life itself.

We're all connected to a higher source of wisdom, power, and service. We don't serve ourselves or others by diminishing our worth; we truly serve by raising our Deserve Level and giving others permission to raise theirs. You have a divine part of your being, and that part is key to raising your Deserve Level and accepting that you are able to create more joy, success, and love.

Self-sabotage is a reaction to unconscious conditions set in motion by beliefs from your past. Your Deserve breakthroughs come through recognizing these unconscious conditions as changeable, as wounds meant to be healed. In fact, you must change them—heal them—in order to transform both your choices and your outcomes. As you embark on this Deserve Quest, you automatically affect the people around you, too: you give them the gift of permission to pivot toward healthier thoughts and feelings.

The Secret, in both book and CD form, has been a worldwide sensation. Its authors have appeared twice on "The Oprah Winfrey Show" and have focused a great deal of attention on the way we create our lives through the law of attraction—and how we need to change both our thoughts and feelings in order to have more success.

However, if your core belief is "I don't deserve it," that core belief becomes an impenetrable barrier, and you must attend to it in order to make a breakthrough. The missing ingredient in *The Secret* is that unless you step across the threshold into *deserving* more, you will not attract more into your life.

There's a moment—a jaw-clenching moment—when something in you says, "I deserve better." It's a soul assertion; a still, small, dignified voice roars, "No more of this!" You can't predict when it will happen, or if it ever will; but when it does, you will feel that "Aha!"

It comes on the heels of your first awareness that something simply *must* shift. After that "Aha!" your Deserve Level starts to go up. It's as though you'd been seeing the problem from a distance, and you now have an instant of crashing clarity. Such awareness is the first step across a threshold and into a new life.

First, you say "I've had it—I DESERVE MORE!" At this point your Deserve Level is exactly what your thoughts and feelings have created. Next, you make a decision and commit to learning something new. If you want things to be different, you must change what you think *and* how you feel about yourself. Integrating those two areas into a new Deserve Level is the breakthrough you need.

In Chapter 12, Self-Talk, I give you the Deserve Affirmations to intentionally focus your inner talk on what you want, rather than what you don't want. This is a basic—as well as a sustaining—step to a Deserve Breakthrough.

In Chapter 13, Self-Release, I talk about the equally necessary process of releasing negative feelings. *Let me stress: you have to address both thoughts and feelings!* The releasing and resolution of old, stuck, hurt, or depressed feelings is critical to any new success or transformation.

In Chapter 14, The Drama Triangle, I talk about the communication skills you need to keep yourself interacting with others on a positive level.

Chapter 15, Self-Nurturing, is a support chapter, designed to help you *keep* yourself where you want to be. This chapter teaches you to be self-accepting even when things are going wrong. It helps sustain your Deserve Level by developing your ability to be self-nurturing rather than self-critical.

In Chapter 16, Self-Support, we explore the place that friends and gratitude have in weaving an emotional safety net for you while you create the life you want.

All of these chapters are designed to give you not only permission to change your Deserve Level messages but also the skills you need to start doing that today.

As with any journey, you have to know where you're starting before you can map your route. The following self-assessment will help you identify your current Deserve Level.

▶ **Exercise: Identifying Your Deserve Level**

Quickly and spontaneously, circle your answers to these questions:

Next year, I believe I will make the following income:

1. $15,000–30,000

2. $30,000–45,000

3. $45,000–60,000

4. $60,000–75,000

5. $75,000–100,000

6. $100,000–125,000

7. $125,000–150,000

8. $150,000–200,000

9. $200,000–250,000

10. $250,000–300,000

11. $300,000–400,000

12. More than $400,000

I believe I can have the material things I want.

1. Never

2. Almost never

3. Sometimes

4. Most of the time

5. Always

I believe I can have a good, loving relationship.

1. Never

2. Almost never

3. Sometimes

4. Most of the time

5. Always

I feel lovable and capable of loving others.

1. Never

2. Almost never

3. Sometimes

4. Most of the time

5. Always

I feel I can produce and perform well at my job or career.

1. Never

2. Almost never

3. Sometimes

4. Most of the time

5. Always

I would rate my love life:

1. Very unsatisfying

2. Unsatisfying

3. Moderately satisfying

4. Satisfying

5. Very satisfying

I would rate my work life (income, work climate, liking of my job):

1. Very unsatisfying

2. Unsatisfying

3. Moderately satisfying

4. Satisfying

5. Very satisfying

I would rate my social contacts and friends:

1. Very unsatisfying

2. Unsatisfying

3. Moderately satisfying

4. Satisfying

5. Very satisfying

I feel capable of getting what I desire from life.

1. Never

2. Almost never

3. Sometimes

4. Most of the time

5. Always

My parents [or you can divide this section to rate your mother and father separately] believe I'm a worthwhile, competent, and lovable person.

1. Never

2. Almost never

3. Sometimes

4. Most of the time

5. Always

Scoring: Add up the numbers of the answers you circled.

> **Less than 20 points: Low Deserve Level.** You don't truly believe you can have much in your life. Take a serious look at changing your thoughts and the statements you make to yourself about who you are and what life holds. You may want to get some counseling; your beliefs about yourself are stopping you from prosperity.

> **21–31 points: Moderate Deserve Level.** You believe you deserve some of life's rewards, though you block the full attainment of these good feelings and events. Some directed imagery and more positive visualization of the desired outcomes would certainly move you forward.

> **32–43 points: High Deserve Level.** You are consistently in line with your positive beliefs about yourself and the world. Keep up the good work. Any hesitations or dips in self-esteem or self-confidence should be treated immediately to ensure continued improvement. You're on the way!

> **44 or more points: Very High Deserve Level.** You are doing everything right, and probably enjoy a great many benefits from your participation in life. No doubt you are a pleasure to know and to associate with, both personally and professionally.

Now you know what your current overall Deserve Level is. The next step to increasing your Deserve Level is to answer this very rewarding question: "What do I want?" Identify where you want to go and what is stopping you from getting there.

▶ **Exercise: The Wants Trackdown**

This exercise requires that you ask a friend to be your partner, Player A. You are Player B. Later you can reverse roles.

Phase One: Awareness

Sit facing each other. Player A should look at Player B and ask: "What do you want?" B should answer whatever comes to mind. A, acting as a scribe for B, writes down the answer. Then A again asks, "What do you want?" and B gives another answer. A writes it down and again asks: "What do you want?"

Do not get sidetracked with comments, agreements, or chat—just repeat the exercise over and over for at least five minutes.

What do you want?

_____

_____

_____

After you have responded many times, look back at your answers. Some of them may surprise you. You may reach a level of wanting—requiring—yearning—that you've never been aware of.

Phase Two: Sabotage Strategies

With your friend, repeat the same procedure as before, but this time the repeated question should be: "How are you sabotaging getting what you want?" Answer this question for every want you listed.

How are you sabotaging getting what you want?

_____

_____

_____

If you find it difficult to answer this next question, don't be concerned. You may not yet know the "why" of your sabotage, but as you continue in this process of sabotage awareness, the answers will come. As we focus on asking the right question, your unconscious will release the information. Your denial system will continue to keep you from knowing until you are ready. Continue with your friend asking you the next question and writing down the answer.

Phase Three: Why are you sabotaging? What do you fear?

_____

_____

_____

_____

_____

▶ **Exercise: Dream It, Do It, Keep It**

This is a simple, three-step formula I use to work with people who want to achieve more in their lives.

1. Dream It

Every external goal starts inside your mind and heart. The first step is to be aware of your dreams and desires. Write them down on a piece of paper; if you do only this much, you will already be ahead of 97 percent of the population! If you don't know what your wants or dreams are, answer this question: "If the best that can possibly happen to me comes to pass, what would my career, love life, health, and so on, be like?" Answer this for every important area of your life. There's your *dream*.

Next, you need to marry your dream of what you want with personal action.

2. Do It

This is the action phase of realizing your goals. Answer these questions to come up with an action plan: "What do I do to make my goals a reality?" "What are the steps?" Write them down as specifically as possible.

_____

_____

_____

3. Keep It

This is the Deserve Level issue. Without permission to keep what you work hard to achieve, you will sabotage it. You can enjoy your achievements and celebrate your victories—or undo them. The next four chapters will outline a plan to raise your Deserve Level and keep what you achieve.

12

▼

Self-Talk

Talk, Talk, Talk

YOUR VERY THOUGHTS ARE THE KEY. YOU CAN DO IT.
WHATEVER YOU WANT, YOU CAN HAVE IT. JUST THINK IT,
FEEL IT, AND MOVE TOWARDS IT, AND WITH PERSISTENCE,
TIPPING POINTS WILL BE REACHED, CRITICAL MASS
FORMED, AND THE MOST OUTLANDISH SERENDIPITIES
ARRANGED.
—Mike Dooley, TUT.com

SELF-TALK IS WHAT you say in your own mind about yourself and the world. There is in your head a chatterer talking to you, day in and day out, about what you can do and have and be. These messages can be helpful or they can greatly inhibit your progress. You are creating your own reality with the messages you repeatedly play to yourself.

Here's the problem: most self-talk takes place at an unconscious level. Just as a computer program runs in the background while you're using it, the very programs that are running *you* are usually outside your conscious awareness.

Our basic feelings and thoughts reside in the unconscious. These early life beliefs, admonitions, and permissions shape our current choices and destiny. It's difficult to grasp the concept of the unconscious mind because no scientific data exists regarding its existence or location. We only know it exists because of its profound influence on our lives. In any major conflict between the conscious and unconscious minds, the unconscious triumphs.

The unconscious mind cannot make a distinction between fantasy and fact. If a person repeats over and over thoughts like, "I'm shy," "I can't make cold calls," "I'm not pretty," the unconscious mind accepts it as reality, no matter what the objective truth is. We constantly listen to this dialogue, and through its repetition we create our reality.

Affirmations

We've all had the experience of energy following thought. Remember the last time you woke up in a bad mood and told yourself it was going to be a rotten day? Proved yourself right, didn't you?

We create our reality by the terms in which we define our life experiences. The classic psychological test to determine if you're an optimist or pessimist is the glass with water at the halfway mark. Is it half-full or half-empty? (Or as a comic once said, "I know my glass is half-empty, I just want to know who's been drinking it!") Our perception creates our reality.

Our self-talk is made up of affirmations—statements we make both to ourselves and others about our behavior, feelings, and self-worth. These statements are so repetitive and unconscious that we don't even notice them.

Some people mistakenly believe that affirmations are only positive statements. In reality, affirmations can be either negative or positive. Statements such as, "I'm always late," "I'm a good financial planner," and "Attractive women never like me," are all affirmations.

If you've been telling yourself negative affirmations, you've been creating negative outcomes. Sabotaging self-talk can be anything that limits you by telling you that you can't have it, do it, or be it.

"I can't win that sales award."

"I just can't handle a career *and* a family life."

"I can't lose that last fifteen pounds."

"I don't really deserve a promotion."

Now is the time to compose the positive messages you want to affirm in your own mind, both conscious and unconscious. By using the powerful tool of purposeful self-talk, you can defeat your unconscious limitations and transform your vision of reality into a new one.

When I'm training my clients to change their negative self-talk to positive self-talk, I teach them how to craft a Deserve Affirmation.

I've heard people teach that affirmations should begin with the statement "I am." Here's the problem with "I am": as soon as you say it, you trip an integrity wire in your brain that says, "No, I'm not." You start your goal statement saying, "I am driving a new car." Immediately you think about the old Honda you're currently driving. When you have a new positive statement and an old negative one together, which will win your attention? Correct! The negative one.

This is what I call the *hidden negative*. When it's paired with a positive statement—even just in thought, without being spoken out loud—the hidden negative cancels all the positives.

Because of this, when crafting your Deserve Affirmation it's important to use a statement your unconscious can initially accept as theoretically possible. Using the words "I choose" gets around the automatic negative response: "I choose to do the work necessary to get my new car." The outcome is the same—having a new car (or job, relationship, or health goal)—yet the focus is easier for your conscious and unconscious mind to assimilate.

This statement also focuses on the process of getting the car, not just having the car. When all of us are trying to envision achieving something more than we have, it's easier to see ourselves in a process of getting it than simply having gotten it somehow.

This step-by-step process still leads to having a new car, but it guards against the mental inner war that sabotages our intent. When doing affirmations, they should be focused on actions ("I choose") rather than states of being ("I am").

The second part of a successful Deserve Affirmation is that you have to believe in what you say. I don't mean "want to believe" or "hope that someday it will happen," but believe it right now. If you're trying to fake it till you make it, you probably won't succeed. You'll end up faking it but not making it.

I do understand that some people swear by faking it till they make it; but I suspect if you looked a little deeper, you'd see they always believed they could make it. You can fake out everyone else, but not that still, small voice in your head. *You* must believe in what you want and are saying.

The third part of an effective Deserve Affirmation is that you have to feel good when you think or say it. I had a client who wanted to win a company trip. She kept telling herself that she and her team had earned the $650,000 level of achievement so she would receive the trip. Every time she said it, she made herself sick! All the affirmation did was remind her of how big a goal that was and how far she had to go to reach it.

She changed her Deserve Affirmation to say: "I choose to give the gift of my business to all the women I meet and enjoy my trip dancing with my husband in Spain." That did it! After ten years of trying, she finally qualified for the trip. Why? Because she felt good and believed that statement.

The fourth part of crafting a Deserve Affirmation is to be as specific and brief as possible. Our minds are cluttered with all kinds of messages, so when we intentionally put in a new one, we have to shape it to be easily remembered.

Crafting Deserve Affirmations
1. "I choose," not "I am"
2. You must believe it at this moment.
3. You must feel good when you say it.
4. The statement must be said with a positive focus. Not "I choose to stop hating my boss," but "I choose to feel good about myself at work."

Many of us think if we just put an "I choose" on a negative statement, it will create a positive statement. *No way!* The complete statement has to have a positive focus, a positive feel, and positive content.

For example, "I choose to stop yelling at my son to pick up his room" is not a new, positive affirmation. State, rather, "I choose to focus on what my son does well and praise him for that."

My New Deserve Affirmations
  1. I choose: _____.
  2. I choose: _____.
  3. I choose: _____.

How to Use Affirmations and Visualizations

First, make your affirmation the new hit tune in your head. Play it over and over. Say it, sing it, anything to keep it at the top of your mind. It took you many years of repetition to create your beliefs, so you need frequency and repetition to change these beliefs to your new, intentional focus.

Put your affirmations on a piece of paper or sticky note on your mirror, phone, desk, or refrigerator—wherever it will help you to notice them, then repeat them to yourself. Put your affirmations on an MP3 player or iPod and listen to them.

Say your affirmations (or write them down) as many times a day as feels good. You can't overdo a positive affirmation or visualization. For visualizations, see yourself in the scene you want to create. Hear it, smell it, taste it, and use all your senses to deeply savor getting what you want. This should be a wonderful experience.

You can't overdo a positive affirmation or visualization.

When I'm teaching my clients how to change self-talk, I use the following analogy, which I heard in an Abraham Hicks seminar:

Let's imagine we're in a rowboat, and we're gliding downstream. The river is flowing with us; it's a sunny, lovely day; the whole picture is perfect. Then we hit a rock, and we turn our boat upstream. Now it's hard, we're paddling against the current, and we're going around in circles and getting nowhere.

Pretend the stream is your career, or your thoughts about your career (or relationships, finances, or health). The more you paddle upstream, the more exhausted and negative you become. The solution is to *notice* that you've turned upstream (by thinking negative thoughts like "I'm never going to get that promotion" or "The boss hates me"). Say **"Stop!"** in your head. Interrupt the negative self-talk, and **pivot** your thoughts toward going downstream (by thinking more positive thoughts like "I choose to do my best and know that the position I want will be there").

The next step is to **savor** what goes right. Fred Bryant says in his book *Savoring: A New Model of Positive Experience* that savoring is the art of managing positive feelings. (In my mind this conjures an image of a juicy steak, a martini, and great friends around me.) Bryant says, "If all you're doing is trying to get by, trying to avoid the bad, you're missing half of life."

People think that taking pleasure in what's good in life comes naturally, but it's really a developed skill. The negative experiences scream for attention, but you have to go hunt for and embrace the positive ones.

Bryant comments, "To heighten your ability to savor and find joy in life when something good happens, you make time to pay attention to it." Then share the experience with others, bring them into your excitement, celebrate your win with them.

Two couples in my life lovingly helped me through the process of finding a publisher. I told these dear friends that when I signed the contract we'd go to a fabulous dinner—and we did! I'll always have the memory of that celebratory dinner in my mind to mark this personal milestone. Bryant says to take a "mental photograph," in which you describe the positive event back to yourself in great detail.

Most of us have no idea how negative our thoughts are. They're like a radio playing in the background, one we stopped consciously listening to a long time ago. It somehow seems more natural to focus on what we *don't* want—on the negatives we want to change in our lives. However, there's a problem with this: we energize and expand whatever we focus on.

We won't stop all the negativity in our lives, but we can control the amount of time we listen to it.

Prescription to Change Negative Self-Talk to Positive

1. Become aware of the negative talk. **Notice** it.
2. In your head—or out loud—say "**Stop.**"
3. **Pivot**: turn toward a more positive thought (your new Deserve Affirmation).
4. **Savor** the positive thought and better feelings.

Emotional Resiliency

We all try to bounce back from certain events that get us off track: the negative comments, the failed endeavors, the career slumps. We had a bad thought or experience, and now we feel depleted, depressed, sick of it all. It's important to keep our Deserve Level high by learning emotional resiliency, because that's how we can bounce back after a loss.

It's also very important to understand that we don't control all the circumstances of such events—bad things do happen to good people. But we *do* control our response to our experiences.

We need our responses to be flexible and resilient so that we're able, as quickly as possible, to return to good feelings and thoughts. Many of us resist pivoting to a better thought as soon as we need to. But once we see we're the interpreters of these thoughts and feelings, we feel more in charge and powerful in our lives.

When I'm talking to my clients, I tell them to view these negative thoughts rather like they approach the issue of doing the laundry. When you run out of underwear, you don't get mad that you have to do a wash, you just do it. It's the same with negative thoughts and feelings.

You are doing an emotional laundry. Use the techniques I've talked about in this chapter and embrace the feeling of being emotionally cleaner sooner.

Heather and Peter's Story

Here's a letter from two of my happy clients, offering their example of how to stay positive in the face of all odds.

Heather and Peter had wanted to expand their small retail business for years:

> *When we'd tell our associates, however, we'd hear, "Expand? Now? Is this the right time? Ridiculous idea—forget it."*
>
> *And that was the "positive, supportive" response we received from business associates when we mentioned that we'd found a new outlet on Maui.*

We own a small tourist-related retail business in Hawaii. "We" being my husband and me. It's our baby, our creative outlet, our passion. As we pass the twenty-five-year marker for doing business, we're thinking back to some of the times our positive attitudes got us through the many minefields of doing business.

We had wanted to spread our wings a bit, expand to include some other tourist areas. We checked out a small mom-and-pop–style shopping center near some of the top resorts on Maui. We repeated the affirmation that we'd used in business many times before: "I choose to find something that no one else can see and make it a success."

"No, no shops are available, nothing at all," was the response of the leasing agents.

We looked around the office and said, "We wouldn't need much space, maybe something like this office."

The secretaries looked at us in amazement.

The leasing agent looked around and said, "Yeah. Why not? We can move this office to a less trafficked area."

And so, we had found our new location.

All of our business associates told us we were crazy; the other tenants in the shopping center thought we were nuts. But we went ahead. We trusted our own instincts, we listened to our own positive self-talk, and we went for it.

A few months later, we opened for business and had the biggest month that shopping center had ever seen. We broke all records for sales per square foot that month. We became a legend.

And then, the following month, we broke the record again when we topped our own sales totals. That store went on to be our top producer, often carrying the whole company on the strength of its numbers.

What if we had listened to all the negativity? What if we had backed down from our inner knowing?

Look for the positive, surround yourself with positive people, keep your attitude positive, trust your inner knowing, and it's amazing what you can achieve. It works.

See It to Believe It

Visualization is a technique that uses vivid mental images as a means to improve performance and influence outcome.

To make your affirmation even more powerful, allow yourself to visualize the desired outcome as you write or listen to the affirmation. Cut out a magazine illustration or take a photograph depicting the things you want. Whether it's a life purpose, an elegant home, a gorgeous car, a happy relationship, or a serene countenance, concentrating on an image will help to reinforce the words.

Put the picture on your bathroom mirror or your refrigerator or your dashboard. Every time you look at it you'll be thinking, visualizing, and reminding yourself: *this is what I want.*

To be effective, affirmations and visualization need to be combined with action directed towards the goal. You can't just passively visualize a desired outcome, while doing nothing about it, and hope to achieve the results you want. Effective visualization needs to be combined with specific skills and active involvement.

The pictures we make in our minds can either help us get what we want or undermine our attempts. Joe wanted to meet attractive women. He faithfully did affirmations about being with and enjoying an attractive companion, but nothing was happening.

When asked about his accompanying visualizations, he answered, "I can't really see anything about her except that she is bored and doesn't want to be with me. Then I see myself standing alone and feeling miserable." His old negative pictures were sabotaging his positive affirmations. He got what he was focusing on—*not* being with an attractive woman.

The trick is to *focus on what you want, not on what you don't want.*

Again, regrettably, we're all trained to think of the negatives first. Because we think of them and feed them energy, we attract more of them. Think about debt—what do you get? More worry about debt. Think about putting on weight—what do you get? More focus on putting on weight. Now flip the negative focus to a positive one. Think about making healthy choices around food and exercise. Feels better, doesn't it? Think about making all the money you need to handle all your financial concerns with ease. How do you feel now?

After he began visualizing a woman turning toward him with delight on her face, and stopped thinking about how no one would want him, Joe felt something inside him change. It's not surprising that he made a connection with a lovely woman just a few weeks later. Find yourself first, and relationships will follow.

Get clear on the things you want, and it is amazing how quickly they show up. Again, it isn't magic! It's a change in perception and in the kinds of nonverbal messages you send out to others.

Affirmation and visualization techniques have become commonplace in the world of athletics, medicine, and sales. The U.S. Olympics sports psychology experts have been using VMBR (visuomotor behavior rehearsal) since the early 1970s. While we know that practice improves performance, athletes have learned that some of that necessary practice can go on in our minds.

VMBR involves fifteen to twenty minutes of relaxation, followed by mental rehearsal in which you see yourself doing your desired behavior as well as you can possibly do it. You see yourself skiing the mountain perfectly, or running the fastest mile, or bobsledding down the hill in the best time. For challenge and variety you can change the scenes or the difficulty; most important is the mental practice and the repetitive experience of success.

In one study, skiers were wired to EMG monitors, which record electrical impulses sent to the muscles, while they mentally rehearsed their downhill runs. The skiers' brains sent the same instructions to their bodies whether they were *doing* a jump or just *thinking about it*. Studies have shown that the athletes who use VMBR do improve their performances.

Similar visualization techniques are being used in the medical field. At the Cancer Counseling and Research Center, started by O. Carl Simonton, M.D., and Stephanie Simonton, therapists train cancer patients to visualize their cancer as loose, unorganized cells and their immune system as a set of healthy, powerful cells doing battle with and defeating the cancer cells. The process is repeated three times a day for twenty minutes at a time, with attention to concrete visualization of the powerful white cells. Highly innovative when it was introduced, the procedure is now widely replicated.

This psychological therapy does not replace conventional medical interventions, but it does augment them. There have been remissions in predicted terminal cases, and in every case the patient has gained a sense of involvement, so that he or she is not just a "case," but a fundamental part of the treatment. One of the most devastating aspects of cancer is the helplessness patients often feel. By becoming involved in the treatment, they experience a renewed sense of power to influence the outcome of their illness.

Many practitioners in the visualization field have found that the best results come from the most detailed and specific images. Sarah, a cancer patient with an interest in the Renaissance, saw her cancer as barbarians attacking her castle; she visualized her white blood cells as valiant white knights fighting for the holy cause. Her cancer went into remission and has remained there for ten years.

In the very different field of corporate sales training, I use visualization techniques to help promote salespeople's self-motivation. I have them place pictures on their desks of what they want: the new car, the trimmer body, the new house, and so on. Every time they make a sales call or pick up the phone, their visual goal is in front of them.

Another helpful technique is to write out your sales goal for the month and post it on your desk or on your telephone. Before you call clients, take a minute to focus on your goal. See that you'll be helping them by selling them your product, and they in turn will be helping you.

Since you're reading this book, my affirmation worked! I have an index card on my desk stating all my goals, and selling this book to a major publisher was number one on the list. This, by the way, has been a goal for twenty years. So tenacity pays off!

Susan Wanted Fun and Success

Susan, a very successful businesswoman in her midthirties, had a particularly interesting sabotage. Having fun was a high priority to her, and she was attracted to men whose most outstanding characteristic was their ability to be entertaining. The problem was that they were all underachievers or unsuccessful in their business lives, and she would end up being their financial support—which eventually wasn't much fun!

Susan had an unconscious belief that a man could not be successful in business and be fun (although *she* was). She went to parties and ended up liking the waiters while ignoring all her business associates.

She decided to do an affirmation that said, "I choose to be with a fun, successful man who is a good communicator." Within six weeks Mike showed up; he was handsome, fun, and very successful.

Abundant Thinking

In my work I've found that most people will take more time to balance their checkbooks or plan their grocery lists than they will to write down what they want for a relationship, career, or health goal. We make lists for everything from laundry to Christmas presents, yet we don't make a list of what we want in our lives.

You had little or no control over the early-life programming that brought you to this stage, but if you choose, you can take control of the rest of your life. To paraphrase Thornton Wilder in *The Bridge of San Luis Rey*, "We either live and die by chance, or we live and die by plan."

You can choose. Through repetition of affirmations and visualizations, you can reprogram yourself to a more abundant life, however *you* define it.

We all want more success, more abundance of all the good things in life. But how do we achieve that? Our ability to have abundance in our lives is more a function of our capacity to receive it than of any limitations on life's ability to give it to us.

We can focus our energy on scarcity thinking, which is based on fear, or on abundance thinking, which is based on love and faith. There's no question which one feels better or works faster.

To figure out which one you lean toward, take a thought about your career (or relationship, finances, or health), and write it out: "I believe that _____."

Then, use the diagram on the next page to trace the progression of that thought through the scarcity line of thinking or the abundant line of thinking. If you find that it's tracking down the scarcity side, see what you can do to change it to being more abundant. The truth of life is that all the success (or love, money, or health) you want already exists. It's your Deserve Level that either embraces it or turns it away.

If you are wanting more and wanting it faster, positive expectation will lead you there more quickly than any other emotion. Choose to believe it's possible to have what you want, and open your head and heart to a feeling of excited anticipation of the outcome.

▶ Exercise: Abundant Thinking

What are you doing to keep yourself from abundance right now?

_____

_____

_____

What can you change to move toward more abundance?

_____

_____

_____

Figure 12.1

SCARCITY (Fear Based)	Energy Flow Change what you feel and think	ABUNDANCE (Love Based)
Focus on lack Not having enough Negative thoughts and predictions		Focus on plenty Having more than enough for everyone Positive predictions
"I can't." "I should." "I won't." "Someone else can do it, not me." "What's wrong with me?" "Yes, *but* . . ."	Language	"I deserve it." "I'm having fun." "I choose . . ." "It's easy." "It's happening!" "I can do this!" "I can handle it."
Tense Worried Harried Frustrated Despair	Physical	Openness Expansion Fun Ease Hope
Comparison Self-criticism Cutthroat competition Judgment	Psychological	Cooperation Trust Being "in the flow" Enjoying the process Acceptance
Winner – Loser Either – Or	Outcomes	Win – Win Both – And
Uptight Being perfect Stuck in one feeling or place	Feelings	Energized, excited Being excellent, not perfect Endless possibilities

13

▼

Self-Release

Let It Go

I know God wouldn't give me anything I can't
handle; I just wish He didn't trust me so much.
—Mother Teresa

There's almost unanimous agreement that positive self-talk is important, but why isn't it enough? Why do millions of people who read a book on positive thinking still not get everything they want?

To answer that question, pay attention to the distinct, though sometimes subtle, difference between *thoughts* and *feelings*. The process of changing self-talk from negative to positive is based partly on choosing our *thoughts*, but no matter how fervently we follow a self-help program, the part that most often keeps us stuck is our unresolved *feelings*. They form a web, and we stay trapped in it.

As philosopher Sam Keen notes: "So long as you do not make distinctions between emotions you will remain a one-feeling person, monotonous like a one-horse town or a one-string fiddle. You will respond to all threats with a single emotion. Love *all* the animals in the zoo. Paint with *all* the colors on the palette." (Emphasis mine.)

In order to increase your Deserve Level, you need to take possession of your feelings as clearly and authentically as you can. When you integrate and honor both your thoughts and feelings, you have complete permission to have what you want.

Most of us do not like to acknowledge our negative feelings. We'd prefer they be gone so that we never feel mad or sad or frustrated or hurt or upset again. But that isn't how the mind works.

You have to express your feelings in order to release them and free yourself of their negative impact. Then—and only then—can positive self-talk really take up residence in your head. Otherwise, your negative feelings will come up on your blind side and do a search-and-destroy mission on your positive self-talk.

In my seminars I use a visceral image about self-talk that never fails to impact people: if you put positive self-talk on top of your unresolved negative feelings, it's like coating rotten hamburger with hot fudge. No matter how good it looks, it will taste awful.

There are two important premises to know about feelings:

- To your unconscious mind, feelings are facts.
- There are only two ways feelings can be expressed—outwardly (released) or inwardly (contained).

Feelings Are Facts

Whatever your unconscious mind feels is an emotional fact of your life and is not up for debate. Yet, because most of us have a hard time accepting certain feelings, we debate and deny their existence or tell ourselves these feelings are wrong. When you tell yourself, "I shouldn't feel that way; that isn't a nice way to feel," or "I really shouldn't *want* to be number one in my company," your unconscious gets confused because it now has an internally conflicting set of "facts."

In this culture, most of us were cut off from our anger early on. We grew up hearing, "Don't raise your voice to me. Go to your room and don't come out till you can put on a happy face." We've been taught to tell ourselves we don't feel anger, which really means we feel it but do not acknowledge or express it. The result: we store it in our bodies, convert it to depression, or both.

The American Psychiatric Association now asserts that ordinary low-grade depression is no longer a psychiatric disorder because *everybody* has it. What a comment about our society—in America it's normal to be depressed! As a culture we have so conspired not to feel, not to express, that all those unacknowledged feelings have turned inward and depressed us.

Believe it or not, anger puts you on the road to your passion. It's the vehicle that enables you to take a stand for yourself. To the extent that you deny anger, you deny life.

Perhaps there were other feelings you weren't allowed in your childhood—sadness, hurt, fear, or even joy and exuberance. To whatever extent you become able to express them, you restore the life energy that has been blocked, and you give yourself a priceless gift.

Tara is an example of the "too nice" syndrome. She got her early education in a very strict school. She says: "Every time I'd say something they didn't like, the nuns would tell me, 'You're ignorant, you're stupid. You don't know anything.' " In her adult life, Tara worked for a major corporation. She was passed over many times for a promotion, was rarely recognized even for outstanding work, and fell into the role of "fixer," taking care of everything for everyone in order to reduce her own pain.

Instead of admitting her anger, Tara covered her feelings by becoming nicer, hoping that she would someday get back in kind as much as she was giving. But the more she gave, the sadder and less validated she felt. What she really needed to do was *protest*! By not saying anything, she was tacitly agreeing to what was happening.

As Tara says, "I didn't feel I really deserved anything, so I tried to be nicer, hoping people would really appreciate me for that." Because her basic needs for personhood weren't being acknowledged, she didn't feel she had a right to more than she was getting. Once she started protesting these personal discounts and stopped taking care of everyone but herself, her depression lifted, and she started to truly feel alive.

Feelings Can Go Only Two Ways: Out or In

If your feelings are not allowed "out" of you, they have to go some-where "into" you. The result can be psychological duress or stress-related physical symptoms—headaches, neck aches, backaches, cancer, heart problems, or ulcers.

The challenge is to learn *effective* ways to get your feelings out—not by railing at your boss or your spouse, or in any way hurting yourself—but by finding other, neutral methods that, once and for all, stop you from shoving feelings back in on yourself or dumping them on someone else.

By releasing feelings in a controlled way—intentionally raising your voice and acting them out—in the privacy of your home and *not* at the person or source of your upset, you expel the toxic energy buildup, and no one but you will ever know what all was stuck in there.

Again, the goal is to express your feelings without hurting yourself or anyone else in the process.

This is the missing part of our emotional survival training. In self-release, the single most important issue is to stop containing your feelings; otherwise you risk edging yourself into a meltdown at the most inopportune time. If you feel hurt, cry. If you feel angry, express it. Find a way and a place to express whatever the feeling is without compounding your problem. Later in this section I'll describe several "release-valve" exercises to help you with that.

You Must Learn to Do Whatever You Have Not Been Able to Do

It's difficult to be authentic with your feelings. In this culture, men are taught to deny their sadness and pain, so instead of acknowledg-ing they have been hurt, they get mad. Women are taught to deny anger, so instead of getting mad, they get hurt, sad, and depressed. But when we don't recognize and own a feeling, it sticks to us with the psychic equivalent of Krazy Glue.

There are three steps you'll need to take to work through your feelings about a person or event: accept, express, release.

- **First, accept what you feel.** You have a right to be hurt, angry, or sad. You don't have to justify your feelings to anyone. They are your "facts" of life. Accept them.
- **Second, express those feelings outwardly.** Talk to someone about them—a friend, a coach, or a therapist. If you just walk around thinking about your feelings but not expressing them, that's called obsessing. You go over and over in your mind what someone said, then what you said, then what you should have said; this kind of thinking keeps re-traumatizing you and leads nowhere.
- **Third, release your feelings.** After you've accepted and fully expressed them (by talking, crying, or protesting, for example), you must ultimately release them. By releasing them you free yourself from the power they have over you and your life.

There's an old saying in psychology: "The only way out is through." You can't release feelings by avoiding or denying them, only by accepting and expressing them. You may be thinking, "Okay, but how can I accomplish that?" This is where dealing with grief comes in.

Grief

All of us have had losses in our lives—love, friends, health, jobs, marriage—yet we often do not allow ourselves to fully heal by completing the grief process. Most people do not understand the necessity of moving all the way through the grief cycle, and thus they block themselves somewhere in it by discounting or denying their feelings.

When I'm coaching businesspeople, one of the insights they come to is that, on some level, we grieve when we don't get what we want: when someone doesn't return our repeated phone calls, when someone rejects us, when we haven't been promoted. This form of grief obviously isn't as strong as when someone dies, but it still has a significant impact. We grieve any loss we experience, so we're going through "mini-griefs" on a fairly regular basis.

In her monumental book *On Death and Dying*, Dr. Elisabeth Kübler-Ross helps us understand the stages of grief through which all of us progress at various times in our lives. I have taken her concepts and added some thoughts of my own to help you understand the stages of grief.

1. Denial. "I can't believe this is happening!" "My marriage is not failing." "My mother is not terminally ill." "I didn't lose that job!" This is the shock stage. You can't believe—can't absorb or assimilate—something you've just seen, heard, or experienced. You deny its reality because it's too painful. "This just can't be happening to me!"

2. Bargaining. "What can I do so we won't get divorced?" "What do I have to do to keep this job?" "Lord, if you'll just let her live, I'll go to church every Sunday for the rest of my life." Like the magical thinking of childhood, this is the stage where you believe there must be something you can *do* to change the loss. On certain occasions, you're right, and you *can* bargain your way out of the potential loss; on other occasions, you simply won't be able to.

3. Sadness. You let yourself feel your pain and loss. You let yourself cry. Your heart can literally ache during this stage. The feelings come and go; you can be driving down the street feeling fine, then a song comes on the radio and you're destroyed. You can be in a business meeting and hear someone say something that reminds you of a poignant moment, and internally you collapse. When you are going through these rapid changes, you can feel crazy. You aren't crazy—you're *grieving*.

4. Depression. This is a kind of numbness; you don't care anymore. You may sleep a lot and find it hard to get up in the morning, or conversely, you may have insomnia. You may stop eating or eat everything in sight. You aren't yourself. You aren't motivated even to see your friends. You lose the experience of joy in your life.

5. Anger. You get mad about the loss. You've lost a business deal or a home you wanted. A good friend, a relative, a loved one—someone—has left you through the finality of death or through the termination of a relationship; whatever the case, you did not want the person to leave. In marriages that are ending in divorce, this stage of grief can be a very painful, accusatory period and can go on for a long time. Obvious or not, anger is somehow involved in every loss.

6. Resolution. You've handled the pain at long last. You can talk about it and feel it without being demolished. This is the all-important stage of integration and forgiveness—forgiveness of yourself and the other person for the pain. This is the point at which you can think of the loss and not be negatively energized.

Everyone in this world goes through grief, sometimes multiple simultaneous experiences of it. Obviously, if you have had two or three losses at the same time, your energy depletion will be substantially greater.

And if you're stuck in any of the foregoing stages, that's the place where you must release. If you're still angry at your ex-spouse, that anger will continue to bind the two of you together in negative chains until you release the anger and forgive. Many couples are legally divorced for years but stay "married" through their anger.

If your feelings can't back up what you want—if you don't have the energy to focus on what you want and deserve—you won't be able to attain it. Several of my colleagues have noted that all therapy is grief work—grieving for the lost dreams, unanswered hopes, and wounded-child feelings in all of us—and my experience would tend to affirm that.

Don Piper tells this story in his book *Ninety Minutes in Heaven*:

> *One of my favorite stories is about a little girl who left her house and her mother didn't know where she had gone. Once the mother missed her, she worried that something might have happened to her child. She stood on the front porch and yelled her daughter's name several times.*

Almost immediately the little girl ran from the house next door. The mother hugged her, said she was worried, and finally asked, "Where have you been?"

"I went next door to be with Mr. Smith."

"Why were you over there?"

"His wife died and he is very sad."

"Oh, I'm so sorry, I didn't know that," the mother said. "What did you do?"

"I just helped him cry."

Rita's Grief

Rita had been very successful building her own business. She had several women working with her and was racing toward a million-dollar year. As she neared this important goal, two of her top performers quit. Not only were these women her colleagues, they were also her good friends. Rita felt betrayed and stayed in bed for three weeks before she called me. She was grieving the loss of her friends as well as the loss of momentum in her business.

As I walked her through the stages of grief, she said, "I'm not in denial, I know what's happened to me. I tried everything I could think of to keep them from leaving [this is bargaining] but it didn't work." I said, "What about your sadness?" She responded, "I've cried every tear there is to cry about this; I'm so depressed I can't even get out of bed!"

Then I asked, "And what about your anger?" She responded with a noticeable increase in decibels: *"What anger?!"*

Rita hadn't thought she should be angry about this turn of events. She'd repressed her anger so thoroughly it had been transformed into depression. As we started to talk about her being angry and about it being okay to let herself protest, her voice became more animated and she started to come alive.

In the next few conversations we had, Rita started to release her grief. She got out of bed and went back to work. She used her new energy to focus on rebuilding her business and is currently one of the top producers in her company.

One of the techniques she used to relieve the pain was to write a letter she didn't send.

Write a Letter

The process of writing a letter (or journaling) can help you move through grief more quickly and more easily. In this letter you pour out all your feelings; tell the person how hurt, angry, and depressed you are and what mean thoughts you've had about him or her. Dump it all onto the paper, but don't send it. Enjoy the feeling of release you have at that moment.

The last paragraph should say, "I choose to release myself from these feelings, and I release you as well." Stating "I choose" is the key to your feeling empowered rather than victimized. Put this letter somewhere only you have access to it, and revisit it whenever necessary.

Self-Release and Self-Esteem

In the book *The Harder They Fall*, gifted comedian Richard Lewis talks about his unresolved feelings and how they impacted his life.

It's hard to know exactly when I became an alcoholic. What I do know is that growing up I felt misunderstood, not appreciated, and in need of validation. I didn't feel I was getting it from important people in my life. They had their problems. I felt sort of invisible.

My father died before I ever went onstage. I had a hole in my soul when my father died. I had already begun to write jokes, but that wasn't filling me up. So I went onstage. Whatever psychological problems I had—and I had my share from growing up—were accentuated being in an environment with so much booze. It was a way of dealing with things I didn't want to deal with. Drinking made me feel not as miserable. It was a great Band-Aid.

Regrettably, the Band-Aid didn't heal the painful feelings or mitigate years of self-inflicted damage. Only working through his feelings could do that.

Lewis talks about the change that came once he got sober and could feel his feelings:

For sure, when the feelings hit home, sometimes they hit harder when you're not high. You feel them full force. But at least I'm able to feel them and be relatively clear. This was never the case before, when I was high and the disease made clarity virtually impossible.

The only way to build self-esteem is to have your feelings and your self-worth acknowledged. If that did not happen when you were a child, it needs to happen now.

For most people, self-release is the hardest issue they'll have to deal with in raising their Deserve Levels. Positive self-talk—learning to say nice things to yourself—is considerably easier.

Feelings are much dearer and deeper than thoughts. You are the only person who can make self-release happen, and you must begin by honoring your own feelings.

▶ **Exercise: Unresolved Feelings**

Take a moment now to write about your unresolved feelings. State what they are, who is involved in them, and what you tell yourself that keeps you from letting them go.

WHAT THEY ARE	WHO IS INVOLVED	WHAT KEEPS ME FROM RELEASING THEM
_____	_____	_____
_____	_____	_____
_____	_____	_____
_____	_____	_____
_____	_____	_____
_____	_____	_____

Release Valves: Exercises for Positive Expression of Unresolved Feelings

It's vital to do whatever it takes to get all those negative feelings out of you. If you feel silly or embarrassed as you do these exercises, remind yourself that those stuck feelings are the source of your grief and are keeping you in bondage, in a prison of pain.

Get Off My Back!

This exercise is done standing, with your knees slightly bent. Your arms should be held up and bent at the elbow so your hands are facing each other. Now, think about the last time someone made you really angry. Think about what this person said; focus on your feelings about the person and his or her statements.

Pull back your arms as if you were rowing a boat, and, with feeling, say, "GET OFF MY BACK!" Keep doing it—at least ten times—until you feel a release from your angry feelings. No wimping out—really make the effort to get them off your back!

Tennis-Racket Release

When some people are angry, they like to lash out and hit things. Because that isn't exactly acceptable in our culture, these people have a tendency to contain their anger until they explode and hit whatever is handy. I know a man who lost control in a rage and smashed his fist into a glass coffee table; he needed twenty-two stitches in his hand and arm.

That's uncontrolled hitting, but this tennis-racket release exercise is a wonderful, intentional alternative. All you need is an old tennis racket and a bed or pile of big pillows.

Mentally place the person you're angry with beside the bed and in a good vantage point to watch you. Now use the racket to hit the pillows with all your power and tell the person what you're angry about. Keep it simple, one sentence or two at the most: "I'm furious that you left me!" "I'm angry that you don't want to have sex!"

Really get into it, say anything you want, and completely release it by whomping the bed with the tennis racket. Find a satisfying rhythm, alternating words with racket smacks.

At the end of this experience you'll have a great feeling. Every time I do it I feel emotionally cleansed. And here's the good news: the other person doesn't even know what I've said. I've released my anger without hurting myself or anyone else, and now I can be centered and rational with that very same person.

Kill Someone in Your Shower (the *Psycho* Release)

This release is performed in the comfort of your own shower. Turn on the water and get your washcloth and soap. Now, think of all the negative things you want to say to the person with whom you're angry. Picture the person there and say anything you want. Throw the washcloth, yell, curse, toss the soap. Then wash off the rest of your anger and step out of the shower, physically and emotionally clean.

Clown Your Way Through

Many people find a good release by laughing away their tensions when they're feeling sad or angry. One helpful way is with the "clown" technique.

Get a big red clown nose and keep it in your car. If you've had a bad day and you're upset and frustrated, get in your car and put on your clown nose. Drive home and casually wave at people as you pass them. You can't stay in a funk for very long with a clown nose on your face!

Tea and Sympathy

If you're feeling depressed or low, one of the best strategies is to have real contact with people you love. Spend some time with your best friend, a close work associate, a family member—someone you can predict will be kind to you and care about your pain.

Talk with her or him as deeply as you can about what you're feeling, and allow your friend to give back love and concern. If your friend's concern shifts into advice, remind him or her that what you most need and want is a caring ear—sympathy and support. The most valuable gift a friend can provide here is to be emotionally present with the person who is grieving. No one has to fix anything; your friend just needs to love and listen.

Make a list of three to five people who would listen to you and care about your concerns; put this list in the top drawer of your desk. Just looking at it can make you feel better.

Forgiveness of Others

Nelson Mandela has said, "Resentment is like drinking poison and then hoping it will kill your enemies."

There's another famous quote about forgiveness: "Forgiveness means giving up all hope of having a better past." In other words, forgiveness doesn't erase the past—it's not meant to—but it does give us hope for a better future. Forgiveness is something we all have to deal with because life events create hurt, disappointment, and anger in all of us. So what do we do when life happens—be angry, ignore it, feel hurt or sad for the rest of our lives, or confront the issue? The healthy response is to confront the issue and forgive ourselves and everyone else who's involved in the event.

Forgiveness is an art and an acquired talent. The reason to forgive is simple: it takes too much negative energy to stay stuck in a state of non-forgiveness of ourselves or others. When we stay stuck, we obsess and revisit the event over and over again; we re-traumatize ourselves and consume monumental amounts of energy that could be used elsewhere for our business and personal lives.

Think of the state of non-forgiveness as a train track between points A and B in your brain. Point A is the incident or person that "started it all"; you take the train to point B, the place where you visit all your hurt, anger, and resentment. But after you've paid your respects for as long as you can, you don't get off the train. Instead, you put it in reverse and go back to point A to fire up for another visit. Until you're willing to forgive, I promise you there will be no shortage of fuel to keep that train running back and forth on that track—but you won't be going anywhere.

How do you know if you have forgiven someone? If you can think of that person without the intense feelings of guilt, anger, hurt, or sadness, that means you're in the zone of forgiveness. Intense feelings keep us connected to the person or problem. The umbilical cord of anger is just as strong as the umbilical cord of love.

Ask yourself these questions to see if you've moved through forgiveness:

1. Does the thought of this person or situation cause me to feel angry, irritable, or depressed?
2. Are there days that I feel stuck and unable to move forward in life, like something is holding me back?
3. Are there people that I refuse to talk to or interact with because of a grudge? Or do I avoid these people altogether? (The exception are people whom you have forgiven but are dangerous to keep relating to—abusive ex-spouses, active substance abusers, or any violent or abusive person.)

Diana's Story

This wonderful account of Diana's journey from self-release to self-acceptance points the way for all of us to forgive ourselves and grow into deserving more in our lives:

> *Breast cancer.*
>
> *It still doesn't seem possible. And it's not fair! How could this happen to me? I don't deserve this! I am too young to face a voracious, life-threatening illness. Me, who loves life! Me, who loves theater, music, dance, and all things magical and divine!*
>
> *Is this why I have gravitated my entire life toward life-enhancing pursuits? So that I could pack more into my life, somehow knowing it would be cut short?*
>
> *A cruel joke, a short life—is that the message? Am I being punished? If so, then whatever for? Is this nature's way of culling the flock, omitting me to strengthen the species? Is it because I don't*

have children, didn't breast-feed them? Does it count that I wanted to, would have loved to?

But that doesn't make any sense; many mothers get breast cancer, some of them while they are breast-feeding.

So is this just existential chaos at work in my life? It doesn't make any sense, it just happened. Is there no way I could have avoided the rubber stamp that hit me? One out of eight women get breast cancer these days. If a line of women walked through the door, the eighth one would be stamped "Breast Cancer: Yes." Was I just the eighth one through the door?

This line of thinking can drive you crazy, I know that.

I feel a welling up of courage or maybe denial, I don't know what it is, that causes me to say out loud: "I am a strong and healthy person with a huge will to live. I will make it through this." Suddenly, nothing but surviving this with our health and love intact makes any difference whatsoever.

One of the first and biggest gifts that I received from the announcement of breast cancer was from my husband, Fred. When we first heard the report from the doctor, we were stunned and in shock. As we emerged from the state of denial and fear, Fred just looked at me with such love and told me that no matter what, this was the only thing that was important. He showered me with the depth of his love, and I just melted into tears.

I began to realize that he loved me, really loved me, without my having to do anything to deserve that love. Even when I was sick, at my weakest, and scared, he loved me.

This information reverberated off my soul, causing a chain reaction of awareness. I began to see that all my life I have felt that I had to earn love. I had to prove myself, work hard and excel, get top grades, and be really productive and successful before I could be loved. I saw that this pattern went all the way back to early childhood, where I felt I had to be smart and entertaining to earn my parents' love.

The issue had run me, all my life. I saw with painful clarity the ways I had sacrificed my own dreams, my needs, my life in the desperate attempt to earn and deserve the love of my former husbands, my friends, my family. And I saw that it has exhausted me, that I was literally worn to the bone with this effort.

Fred's simple act of love and support for me in my time of greatest need ripped off the mask of this deception. I saw so clearly that it was my own lack of self-love that had started the whole series of events. Once I removed my need to earn love, everything in my life was easier, more loving, and safe.

I am sorry that it took getting cancer for me to see this truth, but I am glad that I have been given the gift of sight. I will never again be able to run myself through this same gauntlet. The awareness I have been given is a priceless treasure. I deserve to love myself as much as the other people in my life.

Now that I understand, I can have compassion for myself, can finally forgive myself, and maybe I can begin to learn to love myself for it.

One of the regular ways we can—indeed, need to—practice forgiveness is within our ongoing relationships.

John Gottman, Ph.D., has studied couples for twenty-five years in his University of Washington Love Lab. In his book *The Seven Principles for Making Marriage Work*, he talks about the "Four Horsemen of Divorce": contempt, criticism, defensiveness, and stonewalling. If he sees these four issues existing intensely enough in a relationship, they almost certainly predict divorce. His measurement system has a 90 percent accuracy rate in predicting who will be married fifteen years from now.

Gottman makes the point that all relationships have some of these traits, but the real reason some couples make it and others don't has to do with *repair attempts*. Repair attempts are the ways people try (or don't try) to make up after a disagreement.

As Gottman says, "In marriage people periodically make what I call 'bids' for their partner's attention, affection, humor, or support. People either turn toward one another after these bids or they turn away. Turning toward is the basis of emotional connection, romance, passion, and a good sex life. . . . Many people think that the secret to reconnecting with their partner is a candlelit dinner or a by-the-sea vacation. But the real secret is to turn toward each other in little ways every day."

Forgiveness of Self

Forgiveness isn't always directed toward others; we also need to forgive ourselves. Again, we need to give up all hope of having a better past. Many times we hold ourselves to a standard that's too brittle and, in private, berate ourselves for not living up to it. We take vengeance on ourselves for what we perceive as stupid mistakes.

The problem is that no one knows we're doing this but us. It's our own little secret flogging session. Self-punishment can limit what you accomplish in life, and it definitely lowers your Deserve Level.

But why do we abuse ourselves? The answer is that it's familiar; we learned it from people who abused themselves. And if we don't become aware of when and how we do it, we pass it on to our children. We can change this pattern when we take charge and stop allowing abuse of any kind into our lives, by becoming conscious and restructuring our self-talk and our interactions with others on every level.

How do you go about forgiving yourself? Reassuring yourself that you're loved by family, friends, and God goes a long way toward coping with the fact that we're all prone to mistakes. As Shakespeare said, "To err is human, to forgive, divine." The benefits of self-forgiveness are extensive:

1. It gives us permission to be human.
2. We lessen our fear of disapproval and of making mistakes.
3. We don't waste energy punishing ourselves in private. This private abuse exhausts us by taking away our joy and energy for life.

There are some essential rules for forgiveness:

1. Don't simply "forget" that anything ever happened. You can remember the experience, but don't hold on to the negative feelings.
2. Abandon vengeance.
3. Hold yourself and other people accountable for their actions and words.

4. Show empathy, understanding, and remorse to yourself and others.
5. Ask for restitution, and expect change. Request an apology in person or through your letter (the one you don't send).

▶ Exercise: Forgiveness

Use these visualization exercises to help you forgive more quickly:

Forgiveness Exercise #1

Sit quietly with your eyes closed. Breathe very deeply. Now see yourself going down a flight of stairs. There are thirty steps. Slowly count them down, one at a time, until you reach the bottom.

At the bottom you enter a lovely room filled with a wonderful white light. Take a seat and see yourself talking with the person whom you haven't let go of. Say everything you want to say about your hurt, frustration, or rejected feelings. Take your time.

After you've said all you need to say, tell the person, "I forgive and release you. I forgive and release myself." Visualize the two of you enveloped in the white light, and go back up the stairs in peace.

Forgiveness Exercise #2

Visualize a museum in which the various exhibit halls represent people or situations that have hurt you. Describe to yourself what they look like. See the primary exhibit and tell yourself what major hurt it represents. Go through all the rooms, describing the "hurts" on display. Then walk out of the building and throw a stick of dynamite through the door, blowing it up. Begin your new life.

14

▼

The Drama Triangle

Connect and Communicate

WE HAVE RELATIONSHIPS everywhere—at work, with friends, at home—and when things aren't going well, communication is often a major factor. How does communication in relationships get bogged down?

When communication goes wrong, it's often because we're taking a ride on the *Drama Triangle*, in which—depending on the circumstances and people involved—we play the role of rescuer, of victim, or of persecutor. Most of us tend to gravitate toward one of these roles over the others, but each of us can become eligible for the other two at a moment's notice.

Rescuers are overgivers. They give more than they receive; they don't ask for what they want; they don't say no to the things they don't want; and they don't set firm boundaries. *Victims* are chronically needy people who want others to help them, fix them, or give them direction; they appear powerless, but they really aren't. *Persecutors* are usually rescuers who've given and given and are now feeling angry and put-upon, so they switch into persecuting others. All these roles are dysfunctional and create chaos in our lives.

Once we buy a ticket onto that ride, we can go around and around the triangle for years. This chapter provides the strategies to keep you from buying that ticket in the first place.

The Drama Triangle, the most destructive interaction in human relations, occurs in intimate relationships and friendships, in the workplace and in management. It involves particular kinds of negative communication patterns and role assumptions that are based on collusion and unhealthy dependencies, all of which keep the participants frustrated and resentful. The good news is we're not always in it, and we tend to get into it only with certain people—usually the people about whom we care the most or in whom we're the most invested.

Here's how the triangle looks. When you are in it, there is always the potential to switch positions (see Figure 14.1).

Our mothers told us to be nice, to be thoughtful and unselfish. The Drama Triangle usually starts off with a well-intentioned rescuer

Figure 14.1

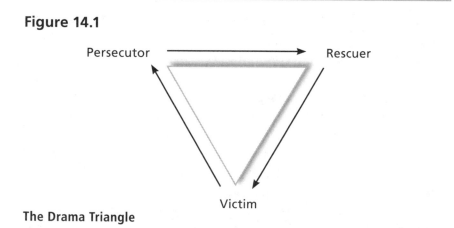

The Drama Triangle

SOURCE: STEVEN KARPMAN. "FAIRY TALES AND SCRIPT DRAMA ANALYSIS." *TRANSACTIONAL ANALYSIS BULLETIN*, 7(26), PP. 39–43.

trying to be nice and thoughtfully unselfish as he or she sets out to "fix" a problem.

Rescuers are people who are overly responsible; they want to help and assist others. Here are their characteristics:

- They are *overgivers*. They give 90 percent to the relationship and get back 10 percent.
- They *don't say no* when they don't want to do things, because they're afraid of appearing selfish. They feel it's their job to be helpful to others.
- They *don't ask* for what they want, because they think everyone else should get their wants met first.
- They *don't set firm boundaries*. They're always neglecting what they need to do for themselves in order to give attention to the needs of others. They don't hold firmly to their own boundaries when those boundaries are challenged.
- They feel *overly responsible* for the needs of others.

Most of us have been trained that it is more blessed to give than to receive. The problem with being in a rescuer position too often is that it begins to feel obligatory. Rescuers do not see an acceptable alternative. Often they don't give because they want to, but because they think they should.

Rescuers tell themselves, "No matter what I feel or want or need, or what is going on with me, I have no right to myself. I am here to help and give to you." And "you" is virtually everyone: husband, wife, corporation, boss, children, parents, friends.

Rescuers are the classic codependents. They feel: "Whatever I need from you requires that I give up something that's mine. I need the connection with you, so I'll give up my needs to keep you happy." Regrettably, all we usually get from these interactions is anger and resentment.

Victims are under-responsible. They need and solicit rescuers to help them and tell them what to do. They're predisposed to be passive and don't seem to know what they want. They tend to avoid taking responsibility for themselves or what they create in their world. They look to other people to make things right for them.

Although victims can be very manipulative, they convey a sense of being powerless, unable to do things or create positive outcomes in their lives. They believe life has victimized them and readily blame others for their own feelings. "He made me . . ." is their emotional incantation.

Each of us is sometimes genuinely a victim of circumstance—for instance, a friend might find that his battery has died overnight and call to ask you for a ride to work. If, however, he has a different broken-car reason to call you every week, he's on board the Drama Triangle. He's not taking responsibility for getting his own car—or life, or financial situation—in order, so he creates a chronic "emergency" and "needs" you to rescue him.

Let's observe the Drama Triangle in action at a family dinner table (which is often where it originates). When I was an adolescent, this scenario happened regularly in my family around the important issue of iced tea.

I put sugar in my iced tea. Dad, in full persecutor garb, glowers and puts me in the victim role: "You're going to die of diabetes. There is diabetes in this family, and you are going to die of it."

Because this happens so predictably, I open my science book and say, "But we're studying diabetes in school, Dad. It says here that it takes a lot more than just sugar to cause diabetes."

Dad completely discounts my source and continues to rant at me about the sugar in my iced tea. He also tells me not to get smart with him.

And who rides in at this point? Mom, the rescuer: "There, there, honey, it's okay, your dad doesn't mean to be angry."

Dad turns on her and says, "That's the trouble with this family, there is *no* discipline, and it's *your fault!*" Mom is now placed in the victim role.

I put on my rescuer costume and say to her, "Come on, Mom, let's go play Scrabble together," and off we go.

Who won? Nobody! We bought a ticket, took the ride around the entire Drama Triangle, and everybody was left with bad feelings.

The irony of the Drama Triangle is that everyone, at one time or another, plays every position. This bears repeating. *Once you buy a ticket into the Drama Triangle, you eventually go around the whole cycle.*

These relationships are based on need. Victims need rescuers, and vice versa. So what happens when victims start feeling better about themselves? One of two things: Perhaps the victim says to the rescuer, "Thanks so much, but I don't need you anymore. I will always remember how you were there for me during and after my divorce, but I'm going off now to marry Harry/Sally." Or else the victim gets angry and says, "I never needed you in the first place. You're driving me crazy. Bug off!" In other words, victims can get angry, which enables them to slide into the role of persecutor and shift the power base.

Persecutors are angry, frustrated, and fed up. Frequently, they're rescuers who've had it and flipped into the persecutor position. When a rescuer moves into being a persecutor, he or she might say, "I'm mad at you, I've had it with you. After all I've done for you, how can you treat me like this?" They often feel quite justified in their anger, because they've overgiven and done too much for the victim.

Now, ask yourself: What happens inside nice people after they persecute? They feel guilty! Guilt then builds a nice road from persecutor back to rescuer, and it's time for another ride: "I was so awful, why did I act like that? This time I'm going to be really nice. I'll give even more, delay my own gratification, and take care of that other person."

The Drama Triangle is the most predominant game of negative interaction in this culture. It's rampant—not only within couples and families, but in the marketplace. When you think of how a number of corporations—to say nothing of small-shop entrepreneurships—are run, you'll be able to write your own scenarios to illustrate the rescue game. The legions of overgiving and underperforming people are overwhelming and financially draining.

I'm definitely not saying that all giving is a game of rescue. When you genuinely want to give to somebody, and you take care of yourself in the process, you're all right. Even then, however, please notice if you're the giver a disproportionate amount of the time.

Rescuers usually rescue out of a sense of obligation, as if it were their consecrated life's work. Ironically, the person to whom you give too much may well end up leaving you for someone else (this applies to business dealings as well as to romance)—or, at the very least, exploiting you. If a real estate agent gives 150 percent to a prospective buyer, that person often ends up buying through another agent. It's often the long-suffering supergivers who are abandoned by their partners in midlife. If you chronically play rescuer, you increase your odds of ending up as victim.

How do you avoid taking a ride on the Drama Triangle? Don't buy the ticket! Staying out of the Drama Triangle is an essential component of raising your Deserve Level. There are four steps that will keep you out of that ticket line:

1. **Give your fair share in any relationship.** Your fair share in any relationship is fifty-fifty. It's balanced and reciprocal; these are the healthiest relationships. Sometimes you have to give sixty-forty, but you should never have to give ninety-ten.
   - *Remember that good personal and professional relationships are a dance for two.* If you're taking all the steps, the other person cannot dance with you. Take a step, then wait and let your partner take a step. Give him or her a chance—don't preempt your partner's move by impatience or your impulse to overgive. If your partner stops dancing, ask, "What's happening? You were dancing, and now you're not." You may need to ask for the reason the other person stopped dancing, or wait for him to start again, or even demand that he dance.

     Many times the healthy response in a relationship is to *not* give, then let the other person respond. The problem with us rescuers is that not giving makes us really anxious. We believe if there's a problem, it can always be solved by giving more.
   - *In personal relationships, don't allow yourself to fall in love with someone's potential.* If you do, chances are you've found an under-responsible victim to rescue: "Surely the love of a good woman will turn him around / open him up to intimacy / help him get sober / show him how good life can be." Rocks have potential! Fall in love with reality!

2. **Ask for people to give back.** This is true in any relationship, personal or business. If people don't give back, they aren't

invested in the relationship, and you need to know that. In sales, there are customers none of us can afford to have. They are the ones who sap your time and energy and never give back by buying; if they do buy, they're endlessly demanding.

3. Say no to what you really do not want to do. It won't turn out well if you say yes when you mean no. Remember Moss Hart's wise words: "All the mistakes I ever made were when I wanted to say 'no' but said 'yes' instead."

The challenge for us rescuers (I refer to myself as an RR—a reformed rescuer) is to keep from saying a knee-jerk yes to everything that is asked of us. We don't want to disappoint others, so we feel compelled to say yes to everyone even when we don't want to do it. *If you find yourself really indignant or resentful toward someone you're close to, you're in the Drama Triangle.*

Ann tells a story that rings familiar bells with many of us. She returned home worn out from a weeklong business trip and was talking with her husband about plans for the evening. She said, "I'm exhausted. All I want to do is be entertained. Let's go to a movie."

He said, "Okay." She suggested a funny movie she'd read about, and once again he said, "Okay."

Sitting in the movie, Ann was happy as a lark with her popcorn in one hand and a Diet Coke in the other, just kicking back. Then she began to pick up vaguely negative vibes from her husband, but decided she'd ignore them and hope they'd go away.

After the movie they went out to eat. All through dinner he was very quiet. She said, "What's wrong?" and he responded, "Nothing." Finally she said, "What is the problem, what have I done that's irritating you?"

He said, "I didn't want to go to the movies, and I really didn't want to go to *that* movie!"

"Why did you, then?"

"I wanted to make sure you had a good evening!"

How many of us have tried to make sure someone else is happy by doing something we didn't want to do? In the process, we made everyone miserable. The "rescue ride" starts out with the best of intentions and blows up in our faces.

4. Set firm boundaries, and don't change them. Your boundaries are the limits to which you are willing to go in any situation. We maintain healthy boundaries with others when we decline to be exploited.

Communication is not just interpersonal (communicating with others), it is also intrapsychic (communicating with yourself). In your intrapsychic communication, you can be kind but firm with yourself about not allowing your old patterns to keep running you, particularly if they are hurting you. That means setting boundaries with yourself, because your old behavior patterns can be addictive—in other words, you feel anxious or "not right" when you step out of them.

Many people I work with are tested on their boundaries by their employers, employees, or children. There will always be those who want you to make a special case for them and get you to think they *really* need extra time, money, or attention. But every time you violate your own boundaries, you make a new "rule" in the relationship—such as, "If the other person is clever and persuasive and needy enough, I will eventually back down."

A Business Rescue

Andrew was a good guy. He loved his best friend, Jerry. They'd grown up together chasing girls and racing cars. Every time Jerry had a new idea for a business investment, he called his buddy Andrew. Andrew, having been very successful—and perhaps feeling a bit guilty that Jerry had never quite made it—always said yes, because he could afford to lose a bit of money here and there.

This went on for years. Most of these investments didn't pan out very well. There was the dry oil well, the land that was located on a toxic dump, and other masterful flights of fancy. But Jerry always seemed so earnest, and for the longest time Andrew thought each most recent rescue would surely be the last.

Then came a final, big "this time will be different" plea from Jerry. He had an inside tip and promised all he needed was $250,000 for this oil-and-gas deal to make them millions! Andrew had been down this road before and really didn't want to do it, but strangely, against his good business sense, he said yes.

You know the end of this story: the deal failed, and it cost Andrew a fortune. The rescuer turned into the victim and shortly became the persecutor. Regrettably, the cost of this ride was a long-term friendship.

▶ Exercise: The Drama Triangle

Write down the ways you've allowed yourself to buy a ticket to the Drama Triangle. Note what roles you have played in certain relationships.

1. At what position do you enter the Drama Triangle—rescuer, victim, or persecutor?

   _____

   _____

   _____

2. What recent experience have you had with being in the Drama Triangle?

   _____

   _____

   _____

3. What could you have done to stay off the rescue ride?

   _____

   _____

   _____

▶ **Exercise: Are You Too Responsible and Concerned?**

1. Do you abandon your routine or work schedule to respond to or do something nonessential for somebody?

   YES   NO

2. Do you feel angry, victimized, unappreciated, or used?

   YES   NO

3. Do you feel angry when your help isn't effective?

   YES   NO

4. Do you find yourself saying yes when you mean no?

   YES   NO

5. Do you feel responsible for the feelings, thoughts, actions, and needs of other people?

   YES   NO

6. Do you try to please others instead of yourself?

   YES   NO

7. Do you feel compelled—almost forced—to help people solve their problems, through means such as offering unwanted advice, giving a rapid-fire series of suggestions, or "fixing feelings"?

   YES   NO

8. Do you take care of others before taking care of yourself?

   YES   NO

9. Do you feel harried, pressured, and overcommitted?

   YES   NO

10. Do you feel guilty about spending money on yourself or doing "unnecessary" or fun things for yourself?

    YES   NO

11. Do you get depressed because no one praises or compliments you?

    YES   NO

12. Do you feel bored, empty, and worthless if you don't have a crisis in your life, a problem to solve, or someone to help?

    YES   NO

13. Do you have a difficult time asserting your rights?

    YES   NO

14. Do you wonder why you never have any energy?

    YES   NO

15. Do you try to control events and people through helplessness, guilt, threats, advice-giving, or manipulation?

    YES   NO

16. Do you ask *indirectly* for what you want and need—for example, by sighing?

    YES   NO

17. Do you push your thoughts and feelings out of your awareness because of fear and guilt?

    YES   NO

18. Do you spend money compulsively, overeat, or wonder why you feel like you're going crazy?

    YES   NO

If you have:

Zero to six "yes" answers: You have minimal codependency issues. There may be an episodic problem, but nothing that can't be solved relatively simply through some focus on yourself.

Seven to twelve "yes" answers: Your moderate codependency issues are complicating your interactions with other people and frustrating your attempts to live life happily. Take steps to solve this problem now before it escalates.

Thirteen or more "yes" answers: Extreme codependency issues are running your life. You're focused way too much on others and neglecting your own self-care. Take action immediately to be more in charge of your life.

15

▼

Self-Nurturing

Where Is the Love?

PEOPLE CREATE THE REALITY THEY NEED IN ORDER TO
DISCOVER THEMSELVES.

—Ernest Becker

MOST OF US point a finger at ourselves or others and say, "That's
how you messed up. No wonder your life isn't working."

That critical, negative voice has a life of its own in your head.

Whatever the ways in which you've been sabotaging yourself so
far, please recognize that those decisions, behaviors, and experiences
were somehow what you needed to do to grow and learn. You didn't
consciously set out to hurt yourself. This recognition can now become
the standard-bearer to your new sense of self. If you pay attention, it
will be the shining light that signals an end to the darkness.

Self-sabotage is your unconscious mind telling you: "Something
in me isn't ready. I need more time, support, or permission to achieve
that goal I so desire." You take a huge step forward when you embrace
that message, rather than abusing yourself for still being stuck. But
how do you do that?

One of the biggest challenges to our self-growth involves learning to nurture, respect, and love ourselves. Too many of us learned very early in life how to denigrate ourselves for even the smallest mistakes and minor errors. Father may have criticized us for any number of things we either failed to do or failed to do correctly. Mother may have accused us of being selfish for not wanting to do things exactly her way. Teachers, friends, and siblings all had their part in pointing out our limitations along the way. Now, as adults, we can take that job away from them because, having studied at the feet of such masters, we've got graduate degrees in self-criticism.

Johnny and Steve and the Puppies

Here's an example of how early we learn to cultivate a self-critical perspective. Four-year-old Johnny is outside playing with his puppy. It's a lovely spring afternoon, and they're having a fine time, jumping around and chasing each other. Like most children, Johnny isn't very attentive to details. He leaves the gate open and the puppy runs out.

He runs to his mother crying, "My puppy ran away!" His mother has had a horrible day handling one problem after another, and this is simply one too many. She reacts angrily: "Shame on you! How many times have I told you to shut that gate?!" Not only is Johnny desolate because his puppy is gone, he's shamed and blamed for being four years old—and he gets an early lesson in self-rejection.

Now let's look at the same situation with different characters. Four-year-old Steve runs sobbing to his mother that the puppy has run away. This mother says, "Oh, honey, that's so upsetting. Let's go see if we can find him!" Steve receives understanding and help with fixing the problem, so he gets an early lesson in self-acceptance.

Both children feel sad about the loss of the puppy, but Johnny is handed the *depression formula*: sadness plus guilt equals depression, the antithesis of healing. If he goes on to put himself down for all the errors he will surely make in the future, he could stay depressed and critical of himself all his life.

Steve also feels sad, but he has his mother's support. She, too, may have been upset about the gate being open, but she was more worried about attending to her four-year-old's distress. Steve is handed the *healing formula*: sadness plus nurturing equals grief, which heals naturally. Whether or not they find the puppy—in other words, whether the grief period is shorter or longer—he'll eventually return to normal, won't be stamped with blame, and his Deserve Level will be intact.

One incident won't make you feel self-critical, but dozens of incidents do generate deep personal doubts and can pitch you toward a low Deserve Level.

The emotional equation looks like this:

FEELS	RECEIVES	EMOTIONAL RESPONSE
Sad	Criticism and blame	Low Deserve Level and depression (Johnny)
Sad	Nurturing	High or normal Deserve Level and grief (Steve)

When we're raised on a steady diet of criticism rather than nurturing, we continue this tradition by treating the four-year-old in us in very self-critical ways. I've encountered clients and friends who are more accomplished critics of themselves than anyone around them could ever be.

Changing Self-Criticism to Self-Nurturing

Dr. Eric Berne has developed a model of human interaction known as Transactional Analysis (TA) to simplify psychoanalysis for public understanding. Berne taught that a person is made up of three "ego states": parent, adult, and child. No matter what our age or life experience, each of us has a parent, adult, and child ego state inside us.

"Shoulds" and "oughts" reside in the parent ego state: "You should brush your teeth." "You ought to exercise." The parent delivers all the instructions and how-to's, along with judgments and opinions. The parent ego state has two different sides—the nurturing parent and the critical parent.

The adult ego state basically deals with facts. Not much emotion here, just plain facts: "How old are you?" "What time is it?"

The child ego state harbors your feelings. When you feel mad, sad, glad, or scared, you're in your child ego state.

If there's an event, feeling, or thought the internal parent deems inappropriate, the critical-parent side pops up with strong negative, self-critical messages: "You're so stupid. How many times do I have to tell you not to do that!" "You're so selfish for wanting that. Stop it!"

We're all familiar with this sort of negative fiction running through our heads when we're self-critical. The child ego state in you feels shamed and blamed, then hurt, angry, and sad. The result is that you feel unable to move forward, and/or humiliated for wanting something, and then just plain embarrassed for having feelings about all of it.

One of the most frequent parental criticisms is that we are selfish or want too much. Some parents label their children "selfish" for their every want or desire. This criticism surfaces for big or little wants, from something as small as a dollar-store toy to something as large as a car. The term *selfish* is used as a club to humiliate or evoke guilt. If used on us often and intensely enough, we can eventually become unable to identify even basic needs and feelings.

So, we grow up, and when we want something, we immediately begin to feel guilty, selfish, and undeserving. We then curtail our simplest wants out of fear of our own—or someone else's—disapproval. We limit our Deserve Level.

Self-nurturing offers the alternative to chronic self-criticism. To get a feel for your own ability to criticize or nurture yourself, read the following instructions, then close your eyes and fantasize for a moment:

Visualize the last time you did something that you wished you hadn't done or that created a problem for you—for example, you locked yourself out of the house, forgot to enter a check, or lost something of value.

Now listen to what you said to yourself. Have a dialogue between the critical-parent and the child parts of yourself.

Do you call yourself names, berate yourself, put yourself down? How is your four-year-old self feeling: Somewhat angry and depressed? Ashamed or hopeless? This is the dialogue that happens when you haven't lived up to your own expectations, when you haven't been perfect.

Now try a different approach. Think of that same incident and see yourself as a four-year-old. Pretty cute kid, huh? This little person didn't mean to mess up. She or he is just learning, or is perhaps a little careless—certainly excusable behavior. Be the child and describe your feelings to the nurturing-parent part of you. "I feel stupid (or sad, hurt, angry, and so on) that I _____." Elaborate on how you feel about the situation.

Then allow your nurturing-parent side to come in and say, "I hear you. I understand that you feel _____. I'm with you and I'll support you. I love you." Continue this conversation for as long as possible.

Nurturing means unconditional support for your being and your personhood. Because it affirms that you're lovable, it raises your self-esteem—and your Deserve Level.

After you've finished this exercise, contrast the bodily feelings you had when you were being self-critical with those you had when you were being self-nurturing. There should have been a great difference in your stress and tension levels.

Let me give you a step-by-step account of learning self-nurturing. This dialogue came from a session with Barbara, a very successful therapist who has helped thousands of people overcome their emotional problems. In her own life she struggles with a phobia about making speeches. This is a dialogue she had between her critical parent, inner child, and nurturing parent. See if it sounds familiar:

CRITICAL PARENT: "Who do you think you are? You can't give speeches! You don't know anything. They'll all laugh at you."

CHILD (CRYING): "I know, you're right. I can't do it. I don't really have anything to say. I'm scared I'll go blank and mess it up."

(BARBARA MAKES AN INTENTIONAL SWITCH TO THE NURTURING PARENT.)

NURTURING PARENT (SOOTHINGLY): "I hear you. I understand you're scared. I believe in you. I'll help you through this."

CHILD (ANGRILY): "I don't believe that. You've never helped me before. Why should you be there now?"

NURTURING PARENT: "I understand that you're angry, and you have a right to be. I haven't been very supportive. I intend to change. I'm going to stop criticizing you and start supporting you."

CHILD: "I don't know. You sound good, but how can I trust you?"

NURTURING PARENT: "Just watch my behavior and give me a chance. You're bright and have lots of valuable information for people. I believe you're very qualified to give speeches."

CHILD: "I feel better. I sure like it when you don't beat me up verbally."

NURTURING PARENT: "I don't want to do that anymore. I love you and want the best for you."

CHILD (HEAVY SIGH): "Thanks."

Faries McDaniel, M.S.S.W., has developed the following model for intrapsychic nurturing. It might feel a little awkward in the beginning, but once you get used to it, it can be used in all kinds of situations.

The Self-Nurturing Process for Decision Making

1. To begin, state in the first person and from the child ego state how you're feeling: "I'm hurting." "I'm worthless." "I'm stupid." Explore and encourage verbal ownership of feelings.
2. After this has gone on for a while, ask yourself what the nurturing parent in you would like to say to the hurt child. It might be something like: "I like you just the way you are." "You're okay." "I'm here for you, I'll take care of you." "I understand how you feel, and we're going to make it through this."
3. Continue a dialogue between the hurt child and the nurturing parent. When you can feel (or hear, or see by your

changed body position) that the child is feeling better, return to the adult ego state.

4. With the child's feelings soothed, assess the situation from your adult ego state. Look at the facts, consider alternatives, and make a decision.

5. From your adult ego state, announce your decision in the first person: "I will do . . ." "I have decided to . . ." By doing this self-nurturing exercise, you will feel less anxious and worried about your decision and more empowered to act on it.

This next self-nurturing exercise offers an excellent way to practice building up your self-esteem. Every night before you go to sleep, grab a pillow and hold it close to you. Pretend this is you as a four-year-old child. Let yourself tell yourself the feelings you're having: "I'm scared and anxious," or whatever. Then see and feel your own nurturing parent come in and love that inner child. This exercise has soothed many a painful night for me.

Nurturing is a learned art. Since so many of us grew up feeling heavily criticized by well-intentioned grown-ups, we became extremely critical of ourselves and of others. Turning these negative patterns around takes tenacity. It also takes devotion to a new practice: not beating ourselves up!

Believing that I'm a good person has helped me stay committed to my own self-nurturing. I'd never try to find in others a level of imperfection as daunting as my own. Once I decided to give myself a break and *nurture* my mess-ups and mistakes rather than be self-abusive, I felt so much better about myself. Consequently, I don't create nearly as many problems as I used to.

Right before completing my master's thesis, I had an occasion to use my newly developed self-nurturing skills. As I prepared to go in and give my oral presentation, panic hit me. What if I couldn't remember anything? What if I failed? What if two years of hard work simply went down the drain in the next two hours!

I was working up a good anxiety attack when I remembered the nurturing techniques. I went into the bathroom, sat on the toilet, and talked softly to that scared little kid in my stomach: "I love you, it's okay. You'll make it through this. They won't kill you." Strange as it may sound, it really helped. I walked out of the stall relieved—and then saw my major professor standing at the sink. She smiled kindly and said to me, "You're right, we won't kill you." Amazingly—or perhaps not amazingly at all—I passed.

Our culture also supports our tendency to see flaws, as well as what has not been completed in our business or personal lives. If you pay attention to the kinds of messages even the most well-intentioned families send—and then add in all the ways the media would have us believe we need to fix ourselves—it becomes clear how we learned to accentuate the negative.

At those times when everything seems to be going wrong, when the good-to-bad ratio is more like twenty-eighty, it's even harder to show compassion and kindness to yourself. The blunt truth is this: if you treated others the way you often treat yourself, you wouldn't have any friends. Fortunately for our friendships, we usually know how to be supportive of the people we care about! The challenge is learning to do the same for ourselves.

It's easy to cheer when things are going well. The challenge of self-nurturing is to love and forgive yourself when things are *not* going well. In business and personal life, one of the best rules for managing yourself and others is paradoxical: *Love yourself when you're down and challenge yourself to grow when you're up.*

This is the opposite of what you usually do to yourself. When success seems out of reach and things aren't going well, it's tempting to tell yourself *you're* a failure. Not only is that approach unkind, it doesn't work; it simply spirals you further down into the cycle of self-recrimination. When the going gets tough, it's especially important to nurture yourself.

This is not to be confused with making excuses, rationalizing, or blaming others. Rather, it's about comforting and respecting yourself so you can lift your energy. When you're doing well, you can challenge yourself to do even better because you have the energy to keep creating. When you're down, you don't.

Remember, we aren't talking about passively accepting an unwanted situation, such as a 40 percent drop in sales; self-nurturing means accepting yourself even when those sales are down.

Telling yourself "I've got to be better, I'm not doing it right, I'm not making things happen," will create negative energy. Accepting where you are means acknowledging your own efforts and energy so you can forge ahead to make the desired outcome happen.

One of my most instructive lessons in self-nurturing came when I made a dreadful error. I was asked to appear on a local TV show to discuss a seminar I was conducting. It was 1979, and the other guest on the program was Barbara Bush. She was beginning a nationwide tour to promote George Senior for his 1980 presidential bid. I dimly knew who George Bush was and had seen a promotional photo of them together, but I was confused about her relationship to him.

She and I chatted for a minute or two, and then I said, "It's so nice of you to go around the country promoting your son for the presidency."

There was a heavy silence, and then she replied, "I'm his wife, not his mother." I gasped at what I'd said and hastily made an excuse that I had to go to the bathroom. I sat down in one of the stalls and tried to put my life back together, because I knew I'd just made the biggest verbal blunder of my life. So I nurtured myself and reminded myself that my intent had been positive. My information was wrong, but my heart had been in the right place.

Experiential Exercise

You can experience the difference between your critical and your nurturing voices with an exercise in imagination:

Close your eyes and pretend that your mind is a radio and you can choose your station. Actually visualize a radio on the table in front of you. Turn the dial to the station you usually listen to. Maybe it's full of self-criticism, or the kind of pseudo-acceptance that sounds supportive but really has a zinger in it: "Not bad, but you ought to be doing a whole lot better." Listen carefully to that same old static that is so familiar.

Now reach out and turn the dial to a new, positive station. Literally see your hand on the dial and feel it turn until you tune in a new station. This one has only positive, nurturing things to say about you—not about the situation, but about you. "I'm with you. I believe in you. You're a good person. You can get through this." Listen for a while to these nurturing, positive statements.

Now turn the dial back to the old, critical station, and check in with your body to monitor how you feel when you hear this station again.

Once again, turn back to the positive station. Breathe deeply. Notice how you feel as you listen to that.

This experience happens in your own unconscious all the time, particularly when you're going into situations that require change or ones that require you to do something different—like grow and develop.

We all resist change. We may want it, but we have trouble with it. As you set about increasing your Deserve Level, one of the important issues is to notice your resistance, your fear. When you start to move toward getting more of what you want, switch that radio station to self-nurturing instead of self-criticism.

Nobody ascends like a rocket—we all take a couple of steps forward, then a step back. To keep your energy going in a positive direction, self-nurturing is essential.

This is not an easy process to master, especially if you've been trained to believe that you will achieve more by harassing and criticizing yourself.

▶ **Exercise: Changing Self-Criticism to Self-Nurturing**

My most self-critical statements are:

_____

_____

_____

I want to change these to self-nurturing statements that say:

_____

_____

_____

Balancing on the Emotional Teeter-Totter

During my years working with people in business, I've interviewed hundreds of successful leaders to discover the key to professional longevity. I've discovered that it boils down to having a balance between *challenging yourself* and *indulging yourself.* If you go too far in one direction or the other, you sabotage your success. But when you're in balance between the two, you're both having fun and making money.

How to Know Which Mode You're In

Here's a simple way to define these polar opposites. When you're in the *challenging-yourself* mode, you're on high alert. You're wearing your business hat, and you're focused on making money and making things happen. In this mode you stretch, reach, work hard, and zoom in on grabbing the brass ring.

There's a danger, however, in taking this mode to an extreme. If you get way out of balance in challenging yourself, you can easily slip into the rescuer role—overgiving to people, then resenting it and moving into the persecutor role. When people talk about being burned out, they're describing a major symptom of being overchallenged.

When you're in the *indulging-yourself* mode, you're wearing your relaxation hat. You're focused on kicking back and pampering yourself. In this mode you recharge your batteries by pulling back from work, reading, doing yoga, going on vacation, and taking naps. The indulging-yourself mode is necessary to avoid burnout, but the danger in staying in this mode too long is that it can become a habit and an excuse for not working.

When that happens, people start taking the easy way out. They slip into the victim role, making excuses for their lack of productivity. What they're really saying is that they've tipped too far in the direction of the indulging mode, but they don't want to admit it.

Keeping the Teeter-Totter Level

Again, to be successful, you need a healthy tension between both modes. You can't focus on one mode at the expense of the other, which is why the most productive, most fulfilled people hold challenges and indulgences in equal measure. When either part of the equation stays out of balance for too long, something has to give. And what usually gives is the commitment to yourself or your business or your relationships.

Maintaining this balance is easier said than done. We learned a life lesson on the playground when we were kids: it's tough to straddle a teeter-totter by yourself and keep it balanced in the middle. To prevent it from tipping all the way down in one direction, you have to continually make small adjustments in your position—in other words, you need to *keep yourself balanced*.

Symptoms of Being Overchallenged and Overindulged

When we're in balance, we're positioned to succeed in life and business. But balance is an *ongoing process*, not a destination or a static state, so it's easy to slip off-center in one direction or the other. To stay balanced, you need to be aware of certain symptoms that pop up to warn you it's time to shift your priorities and recenter yourself. Here's a list of those symptoms:

Signs of Being Overchallenged
- Taking on more than you can do
- Overgiving to underperforming people
- Having too many people pushing you
- Becoming reactive, not proactive
- Sleeping too little; waking up often
- Trying hard but getting poor results
- Feeling guilty and self-critical
- Feeling agitated, anxious, or depressed

Signs of Being Overindulged
- Avoiding distasteful jobs
- Assuming a victim stance
- Not living up to potential

- Using avoidant behavior patterns
- Feeling depressed or lethargic
- Using fear-based thinking
- Sleeping a lot but not feeling rested
- Feeling bored; self-righteous
- Being critical of others' behavior

Which teeter-totter position best describes where you are in your life at this moment? Are you in the *overchallenged mode*, or are you in the *overindulged mode*? Take a moment to place yourself on the teeter-totter. Then think of the key people in your life and figure out where they are on it. This simple diagnostic tool can be surprisingly useful as you learn self-nurturing and increase your Deserve Level.

Balance Is a Process, Not an Event

One of the objections I hear from people who are out of balance is: "I'll make some adjustments when I have time." Well, I'm here to tell you there's no benefit in waiting! The key to maintaining balance is to understand where you are on the teeter-totter and then to make the small necessary adjustments *immediately.*

It's easiest to tilt to the *overchallenged* side, so most people end up there first.

Antidotes to Being Overchallenged
- Celebrate your achievements
- Spend time with loved ones
- Listen to great music
- Take a forty-five–minute walk
- Schedule a night out
- Play hooky for the afternoon
- Rest and renew yourself

When people tip to the *overindulged* side, they let themselves off the hook too easily, make excuses, avoid distasteful jobs, and become critical of others.

Antidotes to Being Overindulged
- You lack purpose: find a mission
- Challenge yourself more
- Set deadlines and higher standards
- Stop making excuses
- Review goals; list your strengths
- Take a calculated risk
- Take bold actions
- Take actions that make you feel good

Given the large task of learning how to regularly nurture and balance yourself, the above antidotes may seem like very small steps, but I promise you they will make a surprisingly big difference in your personal and professional life.

▶ **Exercise: Self-Care and Finding Balance**

Are you currently overchallenged or overindulged?

_____

_____

_____

Go back and review the antidotes so you can get back in balance. What do you need to do?

_____

_____

_____

_____

Now take this quiz to find out just how well you are taking care of yourself:

1. Are you regularly putting yourself last?

   YES   NO

2. Do you take time off when you need to?

   YES   NO

3. Do you have the ability to set boundaries and stop giving?

   YES   NO

4. Do you say no without guilt most of the time?

   YES   NO

5. Do you ask for help?

   YES   NO

If you answered no to the first question and yes to the rest, you are right on track! But if your answers were the opposite, you need to examine just how important your own physical and emotional health is to you.

Tips to Achieve Better Self-Nurturing

1. Take a break.
   - Be able to quit, take time out, or take a minivacation.
   - Stop doing whatever is making you crazy.
2. Do less . . . better.
   - What do you do really well? Do what you love.
   - The most frequent way people get themselves in trouble is trying to do everything. *Do less.*
   - Remember the eighty-twenty rule: 80 percent of the positive outcomes comes from 20 percent of the effort.
3. Rephrase the problem from personalizing it to being curious about it.
   - Take the inner statement of "What's wrong with me?" and turn it around and ask "What can I learn from this problem?"

- Personalizing a problem is blaming ourselves for it, like "What did I do wrong?" The healthier response is, "This is interesting—what can I learn?"
- Stop blaming yourself.

4. Stay in the *now*.
5. Laugh!
   - Make time to have fun.
   - Play a favorite music album or movie.
6. Visualize.
   - Think about a year from now and see yourself in the solution, not in the problem.
7. Do something for someone else. Go help someone!
8. Have good friends and talk to them.

16

▼

Self-Support

Friends and Gratitude Are the Answer

IF THE ONLY PRAYER WE EVER SAY IS THANK YOU, IT IS
ENOUGH.

—Meister Eckhardt

WE LIVE IN a culture where the pioneer mentality reigns. We're trained to be rugged individualists who take care of ourselves and are self-reliant and completely self-sustaining. Many times I've had people in therapy say, "I really don't want to be here. I thought I could handle this myself." These folks believe that seeking help, support, or education is a sign of weakness—the equivalent of admitting failure. Their belief system says they ought to be able to handle everything—*everything*—without ever asking for help.

The reality of life in the twenty-first century is very different. Greater and greater diversification is evident in all areas of life. That means the era of our imagined "total" self-sufficiency is over, and we need one another in order to create an integrated life. This mutual interdependence is the basis for our technology, culture, and psychology. We need support from each other for our very existence.

What do I mean when I say *support*? As children, when we were hurt, sad, angry, or scared, most of us ran to our parents for emotional reassurance and psychological support. If we received the benefits of "good-enough" nurturing, we felt loved and lovable and had an emotional foundation on which we could depend. If this support was consistent, we learned to rely on this source of nurturance, to count on its being there. That left us free to go out on our own, knowing there'd be a safe harbor if we should need to return to it.

The challenge in adulthood is to create support systems for ourselves that draw from several sources, including friends, mentors, and people other than a spouse or significant other. Being another person's sole emotional support is too big a burden to put on a relationship.

To give is to receive. That's the law of love. Under this law, when we give our love away to others we gain, and what we give we simultaneously receive. This law is based on abundance.

This quotation from Gerald Jampolsky's bestseller, *Love Is Letting Go of Fear*, expresses the wonderful duality of support and personal giving. If we give support or love, we then receive it in return. Jampolsky says:

The law of the world is based on a belief in scarcity. That means that whenever we give something to someone, we lose it. We must then constantly be on the lookout to get our needs met. We must search and search to fill our empty well. We live in a belief of emptiness and constant need. We try to fill those needs through getting other people to love us or give to us.

The world's distorted concept is that you have to get other people's love before you can feel love within. The law of love is different from the world's law. The law of love is that you are love, and that as you give love to others you teach yourself what you are.

It's not charity on my part to offer forgiveness and love to others. Rather, it's the only way I can accept love for myself.

Every one of us will hit nights of dark despair, and that's when you need your friends.

Far from being a sign of weakness, asking for and receiving support from others is part of being a deserving, strong, and self-sufficient person. Really strong people value themselves and take care of their human needs. They don't like feeling hurt or depressed, so they ask for support—and aren't critical of themselves—when they need it.

As you build the support system you deserve, it's important to have friends who are living in the ways you want to live. The friends with whom we associate invite us to their level of experiencing life. It's complicated for all of us to be deeply empathetic or supportive of someone whose perspective and lifestyle are radically different from our own. That's why we need affiliations with friends in our particular life phase—friends who can understand and affirm what we're doing and what we believe in, and who can encourage us to become who we want to be. A colleague of mine makes the point that it would be difficult for a fifty-five-year-old woman to go to a twenty-eight-year-old therapist, no matter how impressive his or her credentials and skills might be.

The late Ray Charles said: "I never wanted to be famous. I only wanted to be great." Inevitably, challenge is what impels us toward greatness, but none of us will get there without some resistance from someone, somewhere. That's when a good support system becomes invaluable; it believes in you so completely that you're moved to action.

At certain stages in our lives, though, we do need to assess who in our system is helping us move forward and who is holding us back. Old friends from college can go in different directions from us and develop different values over the years. They may still care, but our life paths are different now—we've simply grown apart. No one is wrong; we're just no longer right for each other.

The same experience can happen in marriages and families. If the people in your support system have become critical or negative about what you want in your life, ask them to be more respectful and supportive. If they're unable or unwilling to do that, you may need to make some choices regarding how much time you spend with them, how much you tell them about what you're doing, or both. Ultimately, we educate other people as to how we expect to be treated. If you allow the people closest to you to undermine your values, you will feel depressed, frustrated, and defeated.

Support Can Change Lives

Chuck Negron was the handsome, long-haired lead singer on the
Three Dog Night superhits "Joy to the World," "Old-Fashioned Love
Song," "Easy to Be Hard," and many others. He lived the life of a
superstar—sex, drugs, and rock 'n' roll. By age thirty he was a multimillionaire; and a few years later, he was living in a corrugated
cardboard box on Fifth Street on L.A.'s raunchy skid row. He had
lost everything and wanted to die.

That's when a supportive friend, Mike Finnegan, showed up.
He had toured with Crosby, Stills & Nash for twenty years and was
a now-recovering alcoholic himself. The combination of friendship,
rehab, and surrendering his wish to die created a miracle in Chuck
Negron's life. He is currently drug-free and touring with Three Dog
Night, still going strong after thirty-seven years together.

The Emotional Bank Account

In his book *The Seven Habits of Highly Effective People*, Stephen R.
Covey talks about an "emotional bank account" that people establish with everyone else in their lives. In place of money, this bank
account uses emotional acknowledgments as currency. Deposits
are measured in friendly morning hellos, thoughtful phone calls,
hugs, sending flowers, or remembering birthdays—anything that
shows people you care about them and your relationship with them.
All successful businesses are based on reciprocal relationships with
others.

Obviously, we all want to have high emotional bank balances
with people we care about. And the more we have on the deposit side,
the more we'll have available when we need to make a withdrawal.

Gratitude

Being consciously grateful for your life, health, career, friends,
and family triggers a change in your focus. I once heard a miracle

described as "a change in perception." Many times when I've stopped to be grateful amidst the hectic pace of things, I've received a miracle of peacefulness that was impossible while I was focused on everything going wrong.

Pure gratitude is one of the best means you will ever have to boost your Deserve Level. Once you start noticing and being grateful for all that you have, you start to attract even more good things.

The grateful heart understands gratitude as a reciprocal process. There's a dance between souls and hearts. We bless the giver with our appreciation, and the giver is blessed in receiving it. William Arthur Ward has said, "Feeling grateful and not expressing it is like wrapping a present and not giving it."

One easy way to apply this principle of gratitude is by using it to change the interaction you're having. Sometimes when my husband and I are getting testy with each other, I'll look at him and tell him three reasons I love him. This immediately changes the energy between us. Then I'll also ask him to tell me his three reasons. When we do this, our focus flips to the sources of our gratitude rather than the sources of our frustration.

Harold Kushner speaks beautifully of gratitude in his book *The Lord Is My Shepherd: Healing Wisdom of the Twenty-third Psalm*:

> *Gratitude is rooted in the sense that life is a gift. The essence of a gift is that it comes to you from someone else, not by your own efforts, and as such is a physical representation of the love and caring the giver feels toward you.*
>
> *A woman who receives a Mother's Day present from her five-year-old understands that the child did not buy it with his own money, nor did he necessarily pick it out himself. Yet she cherishes it as an embodiment of the child's love and wish to make her happy. What mother would hurt her child's feelings by criticizing the gift for being too small or inappropriate? Our gratitude is less for the gift than for the love behind it.*

I think many of us know the joy of receiving a great gift and the excitement of giving a great gift. I had a memorable experience with this several years ago when our beloved dog Maverick died suddenly.

This threw my husband, Steve, and me into immense grief; we spent about a year mourning the loss of our wonderful dog.

As I began to feel some lifting of my own grief, I realized Steve's birthday was approaching. I started secretly looking for a new Wheaten Terrier puppy. I located a litter that had arrived with perfect timing: the puppy I wanted would need the six weeks before Steve's birthday to grow up and be weaned. I was so grateful! For those six weeks, I went to bed every night delighting in the knowledge that this puppy would be my gift to my husband. Guinness is five years old and has been the greatest of gifts in both our lives.

Support and Success: Jesse's Story

When Jesse was a fifth-grader living in Missouri, his year began with his father being taken to prison for writing some invalid checks to try to feed his family. Jesse was left at home with his mother and three sisters. His mother had to work three jobs just to put food on the table and keep a roof over their heads. Jesse's job was to come home after school and take care of his sisters. He'd fix their dinner, help them get their homework done, then get them bathed and put to bed.

Jesse was very responsible and took care of those little sisters without complaining, but it was a hard time emotionally for him. He missed his father and got to see his mom for only about fifteen minutes a day between her three jobs. He didn't have any friends because when the other kids were playing, Jesse was home taking care of his little sisters. At age ten, he had been cast in the role of a single parent. He got quite depressed.

He went to school every day, sat in the back row, and looked down at the floor. He didn't interact with the other kids, didn't know what to say, and pretty much gave up trying.

But he had a teacher who believed in him. Every day as she was working with the kids, Mrs. Skogan would put her hand on his shoulder and say, "Jesse, how are you doing? What can I do for you today?" She was the only person that whole year who touched him, and that touch made all the difference. He stayed in contact with her even after fifth grade.

Mrs. Skogan always made it clear that she had great respect for people with an education. Because her approval meant everything to him, Jesse stayed in school through twelfth grade—which was amazing, given the pressure from home to quit and go make money.

After high school Jesse worked in a manufacturing firm. He learned everything he could, focused, and applied himself with great discipline. He eventually started his own firm and was hugely successful.

Twenty-five years later, Jesse went back to that classroom and sat in his old chair again. He watched Mrs. Skogan do what she did so well, which was love those kids and believe in them.

At the end of the class, he said to her, "You probably don't remember me, but I'm Jesse, and you saved my life. Your love and your support changed what I would have done with myself. I came back to thank you." With that, he handed her an envelope. Inside it was a check for $50,000. He said, "I want you to know that all the love, all the caring, all the support always comes back."

So it is with all of us. When we come to believe and trust that we deserve the best, that trust helps us *achieve* the best—not only for ourselves, but for everyone with whom we have contact. Once we raise our Deserve Level, financial and spiritual success become increasingly integrated with a deep sense of humility and gratitude. We honor those who have challenged us as well as loved us along the way, and we truly look forward to all that we're meant to accomplish in our lives. We operate comfortably from a center of abundance, grace, and joy in the world. In turn, that enables us to love more, serve more, and be more.

And it is at this point that we're able to provide wonderful answers to the question asked by poet Mary Oliver:

Tell me, what is it you plan to do
with your one wild and precious life?

17

▼

I Deserved More and I Got It!

WHATEVER YOU CAN DO, OR DREAM YOU CAN, BEGIN IT.
BOLDNESS HAS GENIUS, POWER, AND MAGIC IN IT. BEGIN
IT NOW.

—Johann Wolfgang von Goethe

ALL OF US want the best for ourselves. In the words of T. S. Eliot, "between the thought and the action falls the shadow." The shadow of our dreams is self-sabotage. The overcoming of our self-sabotage is the challenge of adult development.

Most of the time, we do not simply ascend to glory and goal attainment. We struggle. We take two steps forward and one step back. The hardy and courageous among us persevere to finally reach our dreams. Those are happy days!

I'd like to share with you a few of the hundreds of letters and calls I've received that are cause for celebration. These real people have attended my seminars, or read the book and used the CDs, and have taken the information to heart. I invite you to celebrate with them and to say to yourself: *This could be me!*

Career Celebrations

Getting out of your own way in the workplace can lead to extraordinary breakthroughs and successes. Here are the stories of a few people who found permission to let go of limiting beliefs and sabotage strategies so they could achieve their goals.

Carol's Story

I was coasting along in my business, giving myself reasons instead of results. As time passed I noticed my complacency had become a habit. This chronic *settling for less* was my major sabotage strategy.

I would make an attempt to move my business forward but constantly hit ways that it wasn't happening. I kept saying to myself, "Maybe I'm not supposed to move ahead." I felt weighted down and stuck, and I settled into that experience.

After being introduced to the concepts in *Stop Self-Sabotage*, I had a breakthrough experience; I became aware of my sabotages and started to change my self-talk. I used the affirmation process of saying "I choose," and I stopped putting deadlines that I didn't believe in my affirmations. As I did that, a huge weight came off my shoulders. Then I started teaching others how to use the principles. Because I made this change my business is up over 60 percent in one year!

—Carol Lee Johnson

Mary Beth's Story

My main sabotage involved the *fatal flaw* of *procrastination* and not having a high Deserve Level. When I reached a position in my company, for no apparent reason I began procrastinating—not calling people back and cancelling appointments. I was unconsciously starting to throw away my success.

The reasons I was sabotaging myself were issues I had about prosperity—I believed wealthy people were not nice people. I realized I had to find the truth within myself as to why I was feeling this way and release those thoughts. I came to the realization that wealthy people were like anyone else and could be wonderful and generous.

The information and insight you share in your programs has been extremely helpful with all my own personal bad habits. You have helped me overcome my procrastination and create a business that is relatively effortless. As a top executive in a very large organization, I have benefited greatly from your tools and have been able to lead and coach my team to overcome their own bad habits and sabotages. I use these tools and information with my people daily and consider them priceless. I just love them.

—Mary Beth Relyea

Entire Companies Raise Their Deserve Level

International jeweler Alfredo Molina is chairman and CEO of The Molina Group, based in Phoenix, Arizona. He has become the proprietor of Black, Starr & Frost, one of the most venerable American jewelers during the nineteenth and twentieth century, which crafted historic jewelry for America's "captains of industry" as well as for Hollywood stars. When Alfredo Molina took over as proprietor of Black, Starr & Frost, he became intent on restoring this historic company to its former position, moving forward with the beauty of its past, by raising the Deserve Level of the people in his company. As he says, "The people in my organization need to believe that they are just as important as the people they serve. Once my people understood how they were self-sabotaging and why, they changed their attitude and sales soared."

Carolyn Owns Her Personal Power

Carolyn headed up a quality-assurance department of a major pharmaceutical company. A systematic and precise thinker, she excels at creating quality-control procedures and ensuring that employees follow them. In a senior staff role, she managed employees and, in addition, had extensive contact with contract manufacturers to ensure quality. Reporting to a top management team, Carolyn was expected to speak up in operating review sessions, asserting her contributions with confidence.

Carolyn was part of a group that remained in place after her regional company was acquired by a national firm. That's when all the rules changed. She and her department were now evaluated by a new set of expectations. She is a good listener, concise, thinks before responding, and is respectful in her communication. However, the new, high-powered management team saw her as so soft-spoken she appeared timid, giving the impression of lacking confidence. Her low voice and mild disposition allowed "overbearing" senior managers to intimidate her.

With this kind of pressure, Carolyn became more tactful and diplomatic. Fearing rejection, she consciously rejected others before they rejected her—the very opposite strategy to the one that was needed to survive in the new company culture. As she felt intimidated, she settled for less by giving up on her dream of moving up the management ranks.

Growing up in a small town in the Southeast, she had learned to tolerate control from others even though it caused resentment. She quietly rebelled, becoming defensive and a loner. Digging in her heels, she knew she was "right" and rationalized that they were being unfair and judging her wrongly—a classic self-sabotaging strategy. Relationships with top management continued to deteriorate.

Carolyn was desperate to achieve recognition and secure approval. A friend suggested she take voice lessons to project confidence. Her coach helped her with more than voice projection; he referred her to me to raise her Deserve Level. As she progressed, she began to own her own sense of personal power, quiet but strong. Eventually she changed jobs and found a company culture which fit her personality and pace—one that valued people as much as business processes.

Judy's Story

My Deserve Level sabotage was *denial*. I tend to take a long time because I don't believe I deserve the success. I wouldn't succeed or advance at a reasonable pace because I would be in denial about certain problems. I would avoid situations and act as if they didn't exist. None of those problems solved themselves; it took my conscious and deliberate action every time to break through my denial and deal with them.

Through business coaching and working with Pat, I've realized that I do deserve what I've earned and worked hard for, and I'm more apt to work on solving those problems and challenges rather than avoiding them.

When I first started working with Pat, I was totally depressed. I was still grieving things in my past that I had not grieved completely. I had lost people in my immediate family and in business. My best friend, who had recruited me into the business and with whom I was really enjoying working, suddenly quit the business and moved away.

Pat taught me that when I'm experiencing these painful and powerful feelings, I need to identify them and go through them. Now when I have something upsetting that's happened I don't go into denial, I go through the grief stages.

I turned around my self-sabotage. I refuse to settle for less than I deserve. I am now at the top of my company, enjoying company cars and trips.

—Judy Higgins

Self-Sabotage Makes You Sick: Celestine's Story

I first heard about Pat's sabotage strategies at a seminar for my company. I realized I was using the fatal-flaw sabotage strategy in my life—constantly sabotaging myself with negative beliefs that stemmed from not having permission from my past. I would sometimes even physically make myself sick if I had any reason for not wanting to go out and handle what I needed to do. I was afraid of succeeding because my self-talk told me: "Who do you think you are? You don't deserve _____." My boss would phone me regularly to ask what I was doing and I always came up with excuses—cleaning the garage or in bed "sick."

Once I identified that I wasn't really sick and that I was sabotaging myself, I knew I needed to turn up the heat on my Deserve Level. Pat helped me determine that I also needed permission from my past. The first step I took was to create a recording of my positive self-talk affirmations, which I played over and over. Hearing positive statements every day about the things I struggled with changed my thoughts; I was finally beginning to focus on consistency and actually accomplishing what I needed to do.

The next step I took was to get permission from my past. During one of my sessions with Pat, she advised me to close my eyes, envision myself telling my parents about the successful businesswoman I wanted to be, and then listen to their response. When I did this, my dad said, "You go, girl! Let me know when you reach your goals!" I used to think that it was disrespectful for me to be better than my parents, so it took time to process this new permission, but now I have what I need to follow my lifelong dreams.

Pat helped me make the life change that enables me to follow my beliefs, values, and passions. I extend my sincerest thanks to her for her part in my journey to success. I am now doing fabulously and still keeping her audios in my bedside drawer to serve as constant reminders that I deserve all the success that I bring into my life.

—Celestine Nelson

Chris's Story

In my line of business, communicating with clients is the key to success. I've always been good at following up initially with clients; unfortunately, *initially* is where my communication stopped. I did not realize that my fear of "bugging" people with another call after a few months was holding back so much of my potential. I did not believe in myself or feel worthy of the success that getting their business would bring to my life.

I met Pat at a business seminar, and she changed my whole belief system. Her lessons on self-sabotage and Deserve Level led me to the discovery that I was stuck using a common sabotage strategy: denial. I felt I was doing everything I was supposed to by making those initial calls—that's all I could do, right? Wrong.

I began thinking abundantly—bigger than I could ever have imagined before. I envisioned my sales doubling and really believed it! I learned to flip my negative thoughts before they could affect my behavior. Every day I recited the positive Deserve Affirmations that Pat helped me create.

Since I began utilizing Pat's techniques, my business has done a 180-degree turnaround. Everything has come together: my thoughts, beliefs, and actions. Business is growing and my bonuses have doubled. I feel like no one can bring me down anymore. Not only has my own level of success benefited from this, but as a manager I have been able to pass these concepts on to my team and am a better manager for it.

—Chris Baker

Challenges as You Go to the Top

Sabotage can occur even within a highly successful career. Here's an example of someone who made it, threw it away, and made it back again.

Peter Thomas, the charismatic, wildly successful entrepreneur behind Century 21 of Canada, knows the challenges of maintaining high success levels. At a business conference in Hawaii, a friend told him about the concept of Century 21 franchising real estate brokerage. As Peter says in his book *Never Fight with a Pig*:

> *I felt a rush of adrenaline go through me as I grasped the concept. . . . It combined two old ideas: real estate and franchising. Soon I was brushing off the sand, placing a phone call to Art Bartlett, and leaving the conference for Los Angeles on the first plane I could catch that day.*

Peter Thomas was able to purchase the exclusive rights for Century 21 Real Estate of Canada. He doesn't discount the part luck played, but he says forcefully, "It was not luck that put me on that plane to California to clinch the deal for the Canadian territory; that's called seizing the opportunity. The lucky part was that the timing was perfect."

Within the next few years, there were Century 21 offices from coast to coast in Canada, and Peter Thomas was a multimillionaire. As Century 21 prospered, the ever-energetic Peter got into other business deals. One deal involved guaranteeing real estate for a developer; this venture almost sabotaged his phenomenal success. He inadvertently got caught in a huge real-estate downturn and ended up owing $30 million against his guaranties.

Peter really needed his positive vision and goal-focused attitudes in that troubled time. By using the principles in this book—particularly goal-setting and visualizations—he came out of a potential disaster with his company intact. Peter told me that one of his strategies at that time, when everything was negative and falling apart, was to appoint someone else to take all the angry "where's-the-money" calls so that he could stay positive and focused on creating a good future. It worked! He now goes around the world giving a seminar on how he lost $20 million and made it all back.

Subsequently, Peter sold Century 21 for many millions of dollars and is now using his energy to create and run a nonprofit organization called LifePilot. This organization seeks to empower people to live fulfilling, balanced lives and to realize their highest personal potential. LifePilot was inspired by the tragic death of Peter's son Todd, who committed suicide in 2000. Through LifePilot, Peter promotes leadership through values, engaging people in a dialogue about creating positive change and proactively living their life in alignment with their values. As he said in a personal letter to me after one of my seminars:

> All of us do have our own Deserve Levels. Although mine are about as high as anyone's I know, after your seminar I wrote down some new goals. Did I tell you that after that seminar I walked out and bought myself a new Rolls-Royce Corniche convertible—because, as you indicated, I deserve it!

Brenda's Story

For years I have been challenged with the emotional side of dealing with my business. I begin to get overwhelmed and scared whenever I get out of my comfort zone. I became familiar with Pat's self-sabotage techniques and discovered that I was a perfect example of the *throwing-it-away* sabotage strategy. Every time I got too close to a goal, I would find some creative way to make sure I didn't reach it. Pat's materials not only gave me this insight, but also taught me how to boost my Deserve Level in order to allow myself to do the work needed to reach higher levels of success.

I found the idea of deserve affirmations to be quite compelling, so I began to use them for various aspects of my business and personal life. Unfortunately, I was still not breaking through my barriers. I decided to have a coaching session with Pat to really hone in on what I was missing.

She concluded that when I was doing my affirmations, deep down I did not believe what I was saying. She explained that although I *wanted* to believe my affirmations, in my mind I was speaking a non-truth.

What Pat said about my affirmations tripping an integrity wire in my mind was so true. So many times what I was saying was holding me back because I didn't believe it. Her explanation of Deserve Affirmations and how our mind processes them is what finally gave me my breakthrough.

My business is growing every year and I believe it is a direct reflection of my own personal growth. My understanding of how to handle the psychological aspects of business is carried into every aspect and every challenge I overcome.

—Brenda Wishoski

Cindy's Story

When I began to study Pat's materials, I found that I was self-sabotaging in several areas. First and foremost, I realized I needed to boost my Deserve Level. I felt that I didn't deserve to "win" or be successful. I always felt that until my children succeeded, I couldn't succeed.

Pat's book helped me to determine why I felt this way: my father always gave to his children without ever striving to reach his own goals. He began thinking this way as a teenager helping his mother raise his two sisters. I had learned through my father that settling for less was okay, and I had become resigned to the fact that success was not meant for me.

In the book it suggested we visualize telling someone what we need to do to be successful. I imagined a conversation with my father that immediately brought me to tears. I discovered that I needed to get permission from him in order to move forward in my career path.

This permission from my past, I realized, ultimately came down to a change in my own perception of my father and the realization that he made his choices in life and I, too, have the ability to make mine. I didn't want to settle anymore, and I began to see that I deserved whatever I wanted to achieve with my business.

I set very clear goals to advance in my company and began taking the steps necessary to achieve them. I attended a seminar where Pat spoke, and I read and listened to all of the great information about stopping self-sabotage. I realized how I had been self-sabotaging not only my happiness, but my successes as well.

I began practicing giving myself permission and reassuring myself that I deserved success, and I began to teach my children the same. Six weeks later I reached my goals. I have now set new goals at higher levels and finally I feel that I will succeed—because I deserve it!

—Cindy Hassell

Love Stories

Self-sabotage, because it is unconscious, happens to everyone—even the people who teach others how to prevent it! My story is similar to those of many people who have struggled with deserving to have what they want in all life's important arenas.

Pat's Story: Finding Love on a Tour Bus

I was speaking internationally and traveling ten times a month to exciting places. My income was soaring, but my spirit was depressed. I had gotten divorced several years earlier and was lamenting my single, lonely state. I sat in lovely hotel rooms, watching late-night television, eating Oreos and feeling very negative about myself and men. My self-talk was awful. I'd say, "There are no good men left. They're all dead or married." I knew I was sabotaging myself.

It was then, out of my own pressing need, that I became entirely focused on my Deserve Level dynamics. I changed my negative self-talk to positive and gave myself new permission to believe there was at least one well-matched, lovable man for me in this big world. My affirmation was: "I choose to be married to an attractive, loving, secure man who deeply enjoys life." I also made a list of forty qualities that I truly wanted to have in a husband, such as: he has his own friends; he has high self-esteem and self-confidence; he has a strong faith; he does silly, fun things and is spontaneous. These attributes spoke to how he lived and felt about himself. And then it happened!

On a trip to Alaska, in a tour bus, I met my future husband. I was speaking in Anchorage, and as a side pleasure trip, I took my stepdaughter Heather to Denali Park. We were riding in a park tour bus when we heard an adorable towheaded boy tell anyone who would listen that his dad's clothes smelled bad! He was announcing that they were so dirty they could stand up in the corner by themselves. We immediately began to giggle. As soon as he had found an audience, eight-year-old Timmy gave us the full story.

Timmy and his father, Steve, had been traveling on the train and their luggage had been lost. Several days had been spent in the same jeans and shirts. As we laughed about the perils of travel, I noticed that behind the Dallas Cowboys cap and sunglasses there was a very attractive man.

After a day of panning for gold and horseback riding, we all decided to have dinner together. Tim had told me his dad raced cars as a hobby. I gave Steve the keys to my rental car for after-dinner sightseeing. We were ardently looking for moose when he backed the car into a tree! We laughed about his only going forward on the track.

The next day, after saying good-bye and exchanging business cards, I was driving with Heather back to Anchorage. I was smiling to myself and she said, "You really liked him, didn't you?" I said, "Yes, but he's geographically undesirable. He lives in California, and I live in Dallas. It's impossible to date long-distance."

Coincidentally, twenty-four hours later, in the airport rental-car garage, Steve and Timmy appeared out of nowhere and were walking in front of us. I rolled down my window, and we greeted each other like long-lost friends. At that moment, I heard an inner voice saying, "This man is too important to miss. Pay attention!"

A year later we were married in a seaside ceremony, and I'm the happiest I've ever been.

Health: The Weight of the World

One of the greatest challenges many of us face is in the area of body image. In today's world where "thin is in" and "thinner is inner," almost every woman and many men feel like complete failures if they aren't "perfect tens." And most of us aren't.

A Great Weight Lifted

Here's a letter from one of my clients:

> *I have struggled with my weight for some time and after much agonizing over what to do and which direction to take, I listened to your audios. These CDs have made all the difference in my ability to lose weight and, more importantly, maintain the weight loss. I believe the difference has to do with the CDs helping me focus my self-talk and get clear consistently with my goal to lose weight. Every time I'm tempted to eat that extra cookie or piece of cake I go back to my affirmation of "I choose to be healthy and trim." It keeps me focused on what I want and deserve in my life. I'm out of my denial sabotage strategy and into self-appreciation. P.S.: I've lost thirty pounds so far."*

Finding Success Within

The future belongs to those who believe in the beauty of their dreams.

What does deserving the best amount to, if we're not happier because of increasing our Deserve Levels? That's a question I've asked myself. The answer, I believe, is in this quote from Abraham Lincoln: "Most people are about as happy as they make up their minds to be."

Happiness and quality of life is largely a matter of choice and attitude. Wealth, knowledge, health, and love all help to move us in the right direction. But many inspirational stories remind us that ultimately the human spirit is the final determiner of happiness.

A group of centenarians (people who have lived over 100 years) were interviewed, with some very interesting results. The interviewers found that all of these people shared four traits.

1. They had a positive mental attitude.
2. They were able to handle grief and loss.
3. They had a purpose and a spiritual dimension in their lives.
4. They had a passion and focus on something to do or create.

By getting out of their own way and deserving the best from life, they are shining models for us all.

As George Burns said at age ninety-eight: "I've fallen in love with my future." May you do the same.

References

Chapter 2

Herbert, Frank. *Dune*. Philadelphia, Pennsylvania: Chilton Books, 1965.

Jampolsky, Gerald. *Love Is Letting Go of Fear*. Berkeley/Toronto: Celestial Arts, 2004.

Jeffers, Susan. *Feel the Fear and Do It Anyway*. New York: Ballantine Books, 2007.

Chapter 3

Helmstetter, Shad. *What to Say When You Talk to Yourself*. New York: Pocket Books, 1982.

Chapter 4

Fonda, Jane. *My Life So Far*. New York: Random House, 2005.

Ellen Terry. Interviewed by author.

Chapter 5

Stromberg, Gary, and Jane Merrill. *The Harder They Fall: Celebrities Tell Their Real-Life Stories of Addiction and Recovery.* Center City, Minnesota: Hazelden, 2005.

Chapter 6

Dorell, Oren. "Lottery Winners' Good Luck Can Go Bad Fast." *USA Today*, February 26, 2006. http://www.usatoday.com/news/nation/2006-02-26-lotteryluck_x.htm.

Goodstein, Ellen. "Eight Lottery Winners Who Lost Their Millions." *MSN Money.* http://articles.moneycentral.msn.com/SavingandDebt/SaveMoney/8LotteryWinnersWhoLostTheirMillions.aspx.

"Oprah! (Makeover of the Year)." *People* magazine, March 14, 2005, p. 148.

Thirty Years of Seeing Stars. Special collections edition published by *People* magazine, October 18, 2004, pp. 13 and 110.

"Watergate: The Scandal That Brought Down President Nixon." www.watergate.info.

Chapter 8

Canfield, Jack, and Mark Victor Hansen. *The Aladdin Factor.* New York: The Berkley Publishing Group, 1995.

Pearson, Pat. *Party with a Purpose.* Tampa, Florida: INTI Publishing, 2005, pp. 40–41.

Chapter 9

Clinton, Bill. *My Life.* New York: Random House, 2005.

Dead Blue: A Film About Surviving Depression. HBO Home Video, 2001.

Mayo Clinic staff. "Depression (major depression)." mayoclinic.com/health/depression/DS00175.

The National Institute of Mental Health. "The Numbers Count: Mental
   Disorders in America." http://www.nimh.nih.gov/health/publications/
   the-numbers-count-mental-disorders-in-america.shtml.

Premack, David, and Ann Premack. *Original Intelligence: Unlocking the
   Mystery of Who We Are*. New York: McGraw-Hill, 2003.

Psychology Today staff. "Celebrity Meltdown." *Psychology Today*, Nov/Dec
   1999.

Chapter 10

"About Denial and Addictions." recovery-man.com/denial.htm.

"Addiction: Physical and Psychological." June 4, 2008. http://www
   .fmhsussex.co.uk/drugsandalcohol/addiction/index.asp.

Centers for Disease Control, National Center for Health Statistics.
   National Health and Nutrition Examination Survey. United States,
   2002.

Flegal, et al. *Journal of the American Medical Association*. 2002; 288:
   pp. 1823–1827.

Goodman, Aviel. "Addiction: Definition and Implications." *British
   Journal of Addiction* 85 (11): pp. 1403–1408.

National Institutes of Health; National Heart, Lung, and Blood Institute.
   *Clinical Guidelines on the Identification, Evaluation and Treatment of
   Overweight and Obesity in Adults*, 1998.

"Ryder Addicted to Pain Killers?" *CBSNews.com*, December 7, 2002.
   cbsnews.com/stories/2002/10/24/entertainment/main526831.shtml.

Chapter 11

Tolle, Eckhart. *A New Earth: Awakening to Your Life's Purpose*. London:
   Penguin Books, 2006, p. 109.

Chapter 12

Abraham-Hicks seminar, attended in 2007.

Bryant, Fred. *Savoring: A New Model of Positive Experience*. Mahwah, New Jersey: Lawrence Erlbaum Associates, 2006.

Wilder, Thornton. *The Bridge of San Luis Rey*. New York: HarperCollins, 1927.

Chapter 13

Gottman, John, and Nan Silver. *The Seven Principles for Making Marriage Work*. New York: Three Rivers Press, 1999, pp. 80–81.

Keen, Sam. *Beginnings Without End*. New York: Harper & Row, 1975.

Kübler-Ross, Elisabeth. *On Death and Dying*. New York: Touchstone, 1997.

Piper, Don. *Ninety Minutes in Heaven*. Grand Rapids, Michigan: Revell Publishing, 2004, pp. 193–194.

Stromberg, Gary, and Jane Merrill. *The Harder They Fall: Celebrities Tell Their Real-Life Stories of Addiction and Recovery*. Center City, Minnesota: Hazelden, 2005, pp. 222–223, 227.

Chapter 14

Karpman, Steven. "Fairy Tales and Script Drama Analysis." *Transactional Analysis Bulletin*, 1968, 7(26): pp. 39–43.

Pearson, Pat. *Party with a Purpose*. Tampa, Florida: INTI Publishing, 2005, pp. 77–84.

Chapter 15

Berne, Eric. *Transactional Analysis in Psychotherapy: a Systematic Individual and Social Psychiatry*. New York: Grove Press, 1961.

McDaniel, Faries. Private sessions.

Pearson, Pat. *Party with a Purpose*. Tampa, Florida: INTI Publishing, 2005.

Spalding, Jerry. Personal discussions and writings.

Chapter 16

Covey, Stephen R. *The Seven Habits of Highly Effective People*. London: Simon & Schuster, 2004.

Jampolsky, Gerald. *Love Is Letting Go of Fear*. Berkeley/Toronto: Celestial Arts, 2004.

Kushner, Harold. *The Lord Is My Shepherd: Healing Wisdom of the Twenty-third Psalm*. New York/Toronto: Random House, Inc., 2003.

Oliver, Mary. From her poem "The Summer Day." *New and Selected Poems, Volume One*. Boston: Beacon Press, 1992, p. 92.

Stromberg, Gary, and Jane Merrill. *The Harder They Fall: Celebrities Tell Their Real-Life Stories of Addiction and Recovery*. Center City, Minnesota: Hazelden, 2005, p. 148.

Chapter 17

Thomas, Peter. *Never Fight with a Pig: A Survival Guide for Entrepreneurs*. Ontario, Canada: Macmillan, 1991.

Index

About the Author

In her twenty-five years of experience as a clinical psychotherapist, motivational speaker, and author, Pat Pearson has inspired thousands of people from all walks of life to move through self-sabotaging behaviors and claim their own personal excellence. Traveling throughout the world, she shares the keys to success with some of the world's leading companies, including IBM, Mary Kay Cosmetics, American Airlines, Travelers Insurance, Century 21, Holland America, Celebrity Cruises, and many more.